KILLER POKER

KILLER POKER

STRATEGY AND TACTICS
FOR
WINNING POKER PLAY

John Vorhaus

LYLE STUART
Kensington Publishing Corp.
www.kensingtonbooks.com

LYLE STUART BOOKS are published by

Kensington Publishing Corp.
850 Third Avenue
New York, NY 10022

Copyright © John Vorhaus 2002

All rights reserved. No part of this book may be reproduced in any form or by any means without the prior written consent of the publisher, excepting brief quotes used in reviews.

All Kensington titles, imprints, and distributed lines are available at special quantity discounts for bulk purchases for sales promotions, premiums, fund-raising, educational, or institutional use. Special book excerpts or customized printings can also be created to fit specific needs. For details, write or phone the office of the Kensington special sales manager: Kensington Publishing Corp., 850 Third Avenue, New York, NY 10022, attn: Special Sales Department, phone 1-800-221-2647.

Lyle Stuart is a trademark of Kensington Publishing Corp.

First printing: December 2002

10 9 8 7 6 5

Printed in the United States of America

Library of Congress Control Number: 2002104529

ISBN 0-8184-0630-5

This book is dedicated to every poker player
who ever taught me anything—
and charged for the lesson of course.

Contents

Foreword

Ass backwards! That's right. John Vorhaus wrote a book about poker and he's gotten it ass backwards. But that's a good thing. Just bear with me and I'll tell you why. After all, when John asked me to pen this foreword, he knew he'd have to live with my words, and here they are.

Most of the poker books I've read, including three books about poker that I've written, analyze the game from the outside in. Regardless of whether these books are aimed at beginners or slanted toward skilled, experienced players who show up in casinos and public card rooms to vie for what most people would consider to be anywhere from moderate to pretty high stakes, the thrust of these poker books is similar. They dissect the game from a variety of perspectives.

Most good poker books will teach you what kinds of hands you ought to enter a pot with, and which hands should be thrown away. They'll tell you when a bluff might work, and when it won't. Most poker books will tell you, quite literally, ". . . when to hold'em and when to fold'em," as well as when to raise and even reraise. They even explain poker's surrounding mathematical parameters, from which no player can escape. After all, if one is playing Texas hold'em and flops four parts to a flush, the odds against completing that hand are always 1.86-to-1; as immutable a law as gravity, and one that cannot be ignored by serious players.

In other words, most books are heavily into technique. And for a winning poker player, technique is essential, just as it is for a skilled musician or painter. You can't make do without it. In fact, you probably can't name a discipline in which technique is not an elemental component or basic necessity.

While it may be a requirement, technique alone is not enough to make one a great player. If it were, just reading all of the poker books one could lay one's hands on would make the reader a world-class player, and you and I both know it's not that easy. Something else is needed: a look at the game of poker from the inside out, which is just what John Vorhaus has given us in this book, and he's done it in his usual inimitable, witty—some might even call it eccentric and they'd be quite correct—style.

According to Vorhaus, "*Killer Poker* is more than just a set of strategies and tactics. Mostly it's a state of mind: a state of mind that says I have the tools and skills, the fearlessness and common sense, the dedication and self-awareness to not just win this game of poker but to dominate my foes every time I play." *Killer Poker* takes you there; to this clear and lucid place where you can reach inside and honestly examine how you approach poker. And if that's not enough, Vorhaus shows how to tweak things so that you can start playing the game with a winning, even a dominating, mind-set.

"Go big or go home." According to the author, that's "... everything you need to know to turn yourself into a winner." If "Go big or go home" seems vague or even obtuse right now, you'll have to dig a bit more deeply into this book to glean its true meaning, and you'll have to do the work required to reap the rewards promised in this philosophy. But if you're willing to buckle down and do the work the author suggests—and that means doing a lot more than just reading this book like a novel and then putting it back on your shelf—you can make profound changes of the most fundamental nature in your game.

Of course, *Killer Poker* assumes you are not a beginning player, that you already possess a sufficiency of technique to play the game well. If you don't have your poker technique down pat, then you ought to avail yourself of *Poker for Dummies, Hold'em Excellence: From Beginner to Winner*, or *MORE Hold'em Excellence: A Winner for Life*, and read these books first. I wrote them all and although I'm not above shameless self-promotion whenever an opportunity presents itself, these books will provide you with the basic skills that underpin every winning player's game. Then read *Killer Poker* and let it take you to the next level.

But once you understand the game—maybe even understand it a bit better than you understand yourself—you still have a ways to go. This book will take you there, and you won't be disappointed (although the same can't be said for your opponents), I can guarantee you that.

General Patton once said that the idea of warfare was not to die for your country, it was to get the other guy to die for his. If Patton were a poker player, he might have uttered John Vorhaus's very words: "Don't challenge strong players, challenge weak ones. That's what they're there for." When examined in that context, Patton's tanks and Vorhaus's cards are not all that far apart. All that differs, it seems, is the battlefield and the stakes.

John also advises you that "The only one who can beat you is you." This is not necessarily a new idea, and it's a concept that each and every one of us—poker player or not—should know to be true, but the green felt tables are littered with the detritus of dreams held by players who either failed to realize this or even worse: They knew the truth of this but ignored it altogether.

If you're old enough to remember Walt Kelly's cartoon, "Pogo," in the Sunday papers, you'll recall that sage possum's famous tag line: "We have met the enemy, and he is us." True words, to be sure, even when uttered by a cartoon possum to a gaggle of other bayou critters. And while we're looking for that enemy within ourselves, Vorhaus takes Kelly a step or two farther down that philosophical road by reminding us, "Deception is what you do to others. Delusion is what you do to yourself."

But *Killer Poker* is not simply aphorisms and cotton candy. In his book *Creativity Rules!*, John points out that we frequently find ourselves beset by problems that are too big or too complex to be solved all at once. To be worked effectively, problems must be broken down into component parts. In *Killer Poker*, Vorhaus takes this subdivide-and-conquer approach right to the poker table, where he shows you how to grapple successfully with issues that might appear too all-encompassing at first glance.

This book shows you, in very specific and tractable ways, how to know when you're losing control of your game, such as when a hand you folded an hour ago looks like a hand worth raising with now. "Poker," according to John Vorhaus, ". . . is a delicate dance of knowing when to stick your neck out and when to turn turtle."

If you see yourself in these few, brief glimpses into John's work, then this book is for you. Vorhaus is witty, sage, easy to read, and easily understood. As sophisticated as many of his ideas may be, nothing is arcane. Nothing is obtuse. All that's required to get the most out of this book and to bring the utmost insight and inner awareness to your poker game is to pick up this tome and begin digging into it.

While I may be John's friend, sometime poker opponent, and fellow author, and therefore a bit biased in my view, I know that you'll enjoy reading this book, and that it will improve your game. And you can't ask for much more than that from a poker book. Even if it is ass back-wards. Can you?

Well, actually there is one more thing. By reading this book and taking the ideas and philosophy embodied in it to heart, you'll not only understand yourself and your game better, you'll also know quite a lot about how John Vorhaus plays. But he won't have a clue about you. So if you happen to find yourself in a poker game with John Vorhaus, you can use your newly found knowledge and awareness to van-quish the author and take his money. At least you can try. I plan to.

Lou Krieger
Palm Springs, California
April 2002

LOU KRIEGER is the author of *Hold'em Excellence* and *More Hold'em Excellence*. His following book, *Poker for Dummies*, is now on its way to becoming the top-selling poker book in history. His fourth book, *Gambling for Dummies*, is in bookstores now. He has written more than 250 columns for *Card Player* as well as *Gambling Times, Midwest Gaming and Travel*, and *Fun and Games*. He currently writes regular poker columns for *Card Player, Casino Player*, and *Strictly Slots. Casino Journal Magazine*, the "Bible" of the gaming industry, recently named Lou Krieger one of the most influential gaming writers of the past 100 years, an honor added to only five poker authors. When not writing about poker, Lou can be found playing in the card rooms of Southern California. He lives in Long Beach, California.

Acknowledgments

A poker player's absolute strength is a spouse whose support never fails, win or lose. So I first want to thank my wife, Maxx Duffy, for her unwavering support of my poker habit/hobby/avocation/obsession. I'd also like to thank my siblings and in-laws for never once squawking when I taught all their kids to play hold'em—heck, every family needs an uncle like me. Thanks to my parents who, I'm sure, never thought my college education would eventuate in this.

Thanks to the boys in my home game who think I'm a terrible player, but don't know I'm just playing down to their level.

Thanks to Tom Kenny for coining the word *corking*, and to Pam Scheutz for giving the world *gamnesia*. Thanks also to Bill Bleich, who was there at the birth of Killer Poker, when it suddenly became clear that the answer to every question was, "Raise!"

Thanks to Mike Caro for early inspiration and encouragement. Thanks to Dana Smith for being there for so long, and for generously letting me have my slang back. Thanks to June Field and Melissa Raimondi, two top editors, and to my agent Greg Dinkin, a crackerjack editor—and player—in his own right.

Thanks to you for buying this book. I hope and trust that I can make the read worthwhile.

Introduction

I'm a bully. I'm a bastard. I push people around. I frighten them and manipulate them, lie to them, menace them, pressure them, threaten them, mislead them, outthink them, outfox them, run rings around them in every conceivable way. Then when I'm done—I take their money and go home.

How?

That's simple. I play Killer Poker. Once you've read this book, you'll play Killer Poker too, and then it won't be a question of *will you win?* But rather how wide a swath of destruction you plan to leave in your wake. You will be a tornado at the table. Foes will see you coming and cower.

Can you picture it? Can you imagine sitting down in a poker game with *no fear* of your opponents, no matter who your opponents might be? Can you conceive of controlling that game, no matter what cards you happen to hold? Can you picture people *actually getting up and leaving the game*, rather than tangle with the likes of you? It's poker glory, and it's yours for the taking. It is.

Now, maybe you're thinking, "Right, sure, here we go—another poker book that's going to teach me not to draw to an inside straight. Like I don't have a shelf full of those in my library already." Maybe you do have a shelf full of *those* books—and those are worthwhile books after a fashion. If all they give you, however, are the odds—11-1 against hitting an inside straight—they're only doing half the job. *Killer Poker* gives you something somewhat more crucial than numbers: *attitude*, the psychological weaponry you need to put those numbers to devastating use.

Do you doubt it? Good! It's healthy to doubt, but even as you doubt, I encourage you to *suspend your disbelief*. Contemplate, just for a moment, that there's a better way to go about your game. Imagine that all the strategies and tactics you use in poker—even the ones that *already work*—can be brought to a higher level. Speculate that you just might become a more complete and more triumphant player than you already are. Conceive of a higher mind.

Your evolution won't come without cost. In the course of this book, I'm going to ask you to take some unflinching looks at yourself, and ask some hard questions about who you are and how you now play poker. I will ask you to apply brutal honesty to what you do and why and how you do it. I will insist that you understand your poker in the context of your life at large. You might not like that. You might not find it fun.

Hey, guess what, there's also going to be homework, and you might not like that either. Throughout this book you will find exercises to be done, lists to be generated, and flaws to be considered. You'll be required to write things down. Things about yourself that you might not like to admit. Things about your game that you might not like to accept.

Let me give you an example, so you can see what you're getting into: Thinking about the last time you played poker, identify and describe both the high point and the low point of your session? I'll go first:

> The high point of my last poker session occurred when I
> picked up pocket 10s on the button. I would have raised

any unraised pot, but there were already three raises before the action got to me. I reasoned that I was up against bigger pocket pairs or unpaired high cards, and that I would have to catch perfect on the flop (a ten at least; preferably a ten and no court cards or aces) in order to feel confident about proceeding. Chasing a long shot to the tune of four bets seemed like a bad idea, so I folded. How did the flop come? It doesn't matter how the flop came. I made the right decision for the right reason. That's cause enough to feel good about my play.

The low point came when I got mad at this guy for always attacking my blinds. I tried to be patient and wait to play back at him, but I overvalued a K-T and repopped him just out of rage. Although the flop wasn't favorable, I continued to try to drive him off the hand, a blatant and futile bluff that was rescued by two lucky catches. I let my emotion, not my intellect, control the play of the hand. Even though I got a positive outcome, I played the hand badly and I knew it.

Can you do this sort of exercise? Can you think about your latest poker session in a meaningful and analytical way? If yes, then we'll get along just fine, since it's my job and joy to help you think about poker in ever more meaningful and analytical ways. If no—if you find that you cannot or will not address the facts of your play openly and honestly—then I'm afraid this book can't help you, for *Killer Poker* is interactive in the most fundamental sense: It requires participation from both the writer and the reader. In short, I can't do my job alone. You're going to have to work with me.

You may also have to give up some cherished notions that have served you pretty well in the past. You may be asked to sacrifice something that *works pretty well* for the sake of arriving at something that *works much better*.

There's a problem with this, a problem expressed in the old saying "Good is the enemy of the great." We don't give up on systems that work pretty well. It's only when systems fail that we demand they be replaced. So if you're a winning poker player now, you may be reluctant to turn your back on your winning ways. Even if you are a winning poker player, I put it to you that your *systems have already failed.* Failed to extract the last dollar of value out of your game. Failed to turn you into a primal force at the table. Failed to transform you into the one player that all the others focus on or flee from.

Wouldn't you like to be *that player?*

Then let's get down to work. The exact same work that Tiger Woods got down to *after* he was already a champion. After winning 1997 Player of the Year honors, Tiger spent 18 months retooling his swing. Why? Because he was willing to sacrifice something that worked in pursuit of something that worked even better—and it *did* work—to the tune of eight major tournament wins in 1999.

That's commitment to your game. That's what we need to have.

Yes, there will be cost, but there will be benefit too, and not just the dollars-in-your-pockets benefit that probably brought you to this book in the first place. You'll also derive benefit in terms of balance—in terms of making your participation in the sport of poker generate a positive impact on the rest of your life. In becoming a more confident, winning, keenly self-aware poker player, you will become a more confident, winning, keenly self-aware *person* as well.

Don't thank me. I define myself through service.

In writing this book and presenting this material, I assume that you already have a fair understanding of poker and a decent level of expertise. I assume you understand that A-A is a better starting hand than 2-7. I assume you know that big pairs play better against few opponents and that flush draws and straight draws play better in a crowd.

I assume you know enough not to drink at the table—even if you don't always follow your own good advice.

Why do I assume these things? Because this book is not an introductory guide to poker. It's for people looking to deepen their understanding of the game and looking to take their game to successively higher levels. Let's look at it this way: Poker is an onion; your comprehension of the game improves as you peel back the layers. This book assumes that the skin has long since been removed and washed down the drain. Now we're somewhere between the outer layers and the core, moving deeper, ever deeper, toward the heart of poker understanding.

Most of the examples and practical exercises in this book involve limit hold'em, because that's what most of us play. You'll find some references to Omaha/8 and a smattering of stud, but mostly it's hold'em, hold'em, hold'em, and why not? Texas hold'em is now the single most popular form of poker in the world and the game that is used to determine the World Series of Poker champion. The underlying principles apply to all forms of poker, so extrapolate according to your need. Whether you're playing lowball in an old-growth California card room or Spit in the Ocean at your kitchen table, the underlying mind-set of Killer Poker applies: Whatever your goal once was, you now have a new goal. To *dominate* and *crush* your opponents. It seems like such a small thing, but in reality, it's the world—the world of Killer Poker.

The mass of men lead lives of quiet
desperation.
—Henry David Thoreau

Now, let's play poker.
—Linda Johnson

KILLER POKER

1

♣ ♠ ♦ ♥

WHAT IS KILLER POKER?

♧ ♤ ◇ ♡

Killer Poker is more than just a set of strategies and tactics. Mostly it's state of mind: a state of mind that says, "I have the tools and skills, the fearlessness and common sense, the dedication and self-awareness not just to win this game of poker but to *dominate* my foes every time I play." That's it in a nutshell.

Of course, there's a little more to it than that.

RAISE

Imagine that you're playing poker. That's not hard, is it? Not for people like you who spend every waking hour playing poker, thinking about poker, or looking for ways to improve your play. How do I know this about you? That's simple: I know what you're thinking. It's true. I know what you're thinking at the table. I know what you're thinking away from the table. I know what you're thinking when you're driving down the ol' [insert name of local highway here] to [insert name of local card club here] to play a little $2–$4, $4–$8, $3–$6, $6–$12 with a kill, $10–$20, $20–$40 hold'em, Omaha, lowball, or stud. Know how I know?

That's easy: I can read minds. Once I learned to read mine, yours was a snap.

Don't worry; I'll teach you how to read minds too. It's just part of what I know about Killer Poker, and I plan to teach you *everything* I know about Killer Poker. Eventually you'll have all my secrets: how to read minds, instill dread, play like a(n apparent) maniac, and win. Are you impatient? Do you want it all at once, all the wisdom, all the glory, all the art and science of Killer Poker? Okay, here it is:

> *Go big or go home.*

There—there it is—everything you need to know to turn yourself into a winner. Go big or go home.

Do you want more? Okay, here it comes.

Imagine that you're playing poker, but imagine that you're also playing a secret game called "Raise!" where the object of the game is to raise as much as possible—the more raises you make the higher your score. To your enemies, your actions would look reckless, a mistake, but according to your hidden rules, you're playing exactly correctly—a winning strategy in a completely different game. That's the secret and that's the wisdom. To play Killer Poker, you play *exactly correctly* according to your own hidden rules.

Think it through. Think of all the drones around you playing poker by the book. They raise with big cards and fold with small ones. They don't get out of line. They don't *want* to get out of line and they *don't want you to either*. They want a nice, safe, congenial, cooperative game of poker. Their tightness and their discipline seem like assets, but you know what? That tightness is a straitjacket and that discipline can be too.

Think about who really wins in these games. I'm not talking about small wins, a smattering of dollars to the good. I'm talking about *big* wins: "get a hernia carrying your racks to the cage" wins. Who gets those? The bold and the dominant, that's who, the bullies. It's people who play by their own rules. It's players who have a feral determination to slaughter everyone in sight. That can be you. It can—once you have that same boldness and dominance, that imagination, and that determination to win.

You've been weak up till now. That can end. You've been timid up till now. That can end. You've been conservative, fearful, restless, inattentive, tyrannized, exploited, shot, stabbed, and killed up till now—but that can end! All you have to do is open your mind and let change wash over you.

As you know, there are four basic states of play in poker: Weak, Strong, Tight, and Loose (plus combinations in between: Weak-Tight, Weak-Loose, Strong-Tight, and Strong-Loose). For your convenience, I present these states in compass form (see next page).

Before we go further, ask yourself this hard question: Where on the compass are you? Not "where would you like to be?" Or "where do you hope to be?" But where, in actual factual fact, are you now? Be honest. We won't get anywhere if you're not honest.

"My basic state of poker is: _____."

That's good. You've told the truth to yourself about yourself. That's an excellent start for what we're trying to accomplish here.

Now here's the thing, a thing you probably already know: You can't win weak-tight and you can't win weak-loose. You just can't. Weak in any form won't get it done. So that means, flat out, that you must stop being weak right now. You must never play weak poker again. You must play strong, all the time, every time. Strong-loose (or at least the *appearance* of loose) or strong-tight, it doesn't matter—so

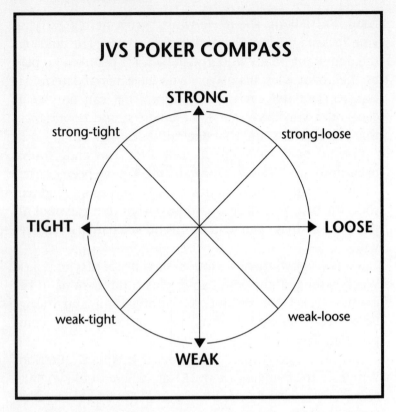

long as you play strong. That's what we mean when we say go big or go home.

You're not sure you want to play strong, are you? Or no, you *want* to play strong, but you're afraid. You tried playing strong once and it was an absolute disaster. Trouble is, you weren't playing strong. You only thought you were. You may have been a bit more aggressive than usual, but you were still playing hard-hat poker—safety first! You raised with big pairs, threw away junk, and flat-called with drawing hands to encourage callers and get the proper odds, and so on. That's an okay strategy, even a winning strategy—if the cards fall your way. Wouldn't you rather be able to win no matter how the cards fall? The best players can. They do it every day. You can, too, but it's going to take transformation. Are you up for that? Are you ready to be born again?

I'm not sure that you are. I'm not sure you're interested in risk at all. Do you know how I know? Because I'm not either. I have had to drag myself kicking and screaming to the Killer Poker mind-set. It does not come naturally to walk into a public card room and think, "Now I shall wreak havoc." Yet that's what's required. I know this. I have proof in my wallet. You can have it, too, if you want.

But you know what? I'm being coy, and why should I bother being coy? I don't have to build you a comfortable home here. All I have to do is put this information out there and let you make of it what you will. The truth is revealed under pressure. If you like pressure, you'll stay; if you don't you'll leave. You will, in short, go big or go home. It's your call.

Or should I say raise?

> *During your next session, commit to making an opening raise five or more hands in a row. Don't worry about the outcome, but do note the effect of your aggressive play on your opponents.*

LIARESE

"Tightness is a straitjacket, and discipline can be too." It's a shocking notion, no? It flies in the face of everything we've been taught. Tight poker is *winning* poker, right? Everyone knows that. And discipline, well, discipline is the rock upon which the church of poker is built, right? *Not exactly*.

Tightness and discipline work for you if they're the *truth* of your play. Too often, though, they're just the rationalization we cook up for the mess we make of our playing sessions. "I played tight," we say, "I played with discipline. I can't understand why I lost." It's not that we can't *understand*, it's rather that we can't *admit*. We hide our denial behind the claim that we played kosher poker, which somehow excuses our sins.

Hey, if you're going to play Killer Poker, the first thing you have to do is get over your lies and confess your sins. I won't make your list for you—there will be plenty of time for list making later—but I will encourage you to think about the lies you have told in defense of your own bad play. Here are two examples:

You're playing in the late stage of a hold'em tournament and a player raises before the flop. You call the raise holding Q-T. You figure that your foe has something like a pair of 9s, and he does. Your heart is gladdened by a queen on the flop, but then your foe catches that miracle nine for a set on the turn or the river. Your stack is emasculated, and you never recover. Soon you're in the parking lot, heading home.

You call this a bad beat, but it's not—not really. Your hand wasn't the favorite to start. You went a little ahead on the flop, but your foe took his rightful place in the lead on the turn or the river. You *lied to yourself* about the real strength of your hand.

Here's the second example, also in a tournament late-stage:

Now you have the pocket nines. Before the action gets to you, one player has raised and a second player has called. You feel disappointment because you had planned to raise with your pocket nines, but now these bohos have stolen your thunder. It occurs to you that, while they both might have bigger pairs than yours, they might also both have premium nonpaired hands like A-K, in which case their A-Ks are seemingly neutralizing one another and giving you a big fat edge.

Anyway, that's what you tell yourself. All you're really doing is rationalizing a bad call, because the fact is that both these players are on big pairs, and you know it. Only you don't admit it, because you'd rather stick to your lie and live with your delusion than admit the truth that your pocket nines must go in the muck. The truth is that you're more interested in the action than being a favorite in the pot—a great way to be eliminated in tournament play.

Lies just get in the way. So let's get over our lies.

The Lies We Tell Ourselves

Losers speak a certain language, one that requires deft and careful translation. If you pay close attention you can learn to speak *liarese*. Just study the following:

What They Say	What They Mean
"I came out a little ahead."	"I lost."
"I broke even."	"I lost."
"I dropped a few bucks."	"I lost."
"I couldn't catch a card."	"I lost."
"I had a good time."	"I lost."

Losers are liars. You can't trust 'em. It's bad enough that they lie to you (they swear to God they'll pay you back), but oh the lies that they tell themselves. Let's crawl inside a loser's head and hear what he has to say. Don't forget your translation key above.

- "I didn't play too badly tonight." ("I lost.")
- "I couldn't catch a damn flop; that's for sure." ("I lost.")

- "You just can't protect your hand at a betting limit this low." ("I lost.")
- "I should play higher."

Hey now, there's a handy lie: *"I should play higher."* Yeeps! No sooner has this chucklehead's game degenerated to denial of what he just went through than he's out there looking for an excuse to do it to himself again—and worse. You see it all the time.

A loser gets hammered out of a game. What does he do next? Does he look at himself dispassionately and say, "I guess I should absorb my loss and just go home. Clearly I'm off my game tonight." As if! As if that terribly useful thought ever crossed his mind. Instead of looking at himself, he looks around the card room and notices an open seat in a higher limit game—and I mean a much higher limit, the limit that makes him go *gulp!*

We'll get back to this loser and his problems in a minute, but first I want to ask you a question: *What's your gulp limit?* At what point do the stakes of the game start to have meaning for you? $1–$2? $100–$200? $1,000–$2,000? What? Everyone's gulp limit is different. Grandma goes gulp at the sight of quarters on the kitchen table. Some don't go gulp at Fort Knox. So what's your gulp limit and why? For someone the answer might be this: "I go gulp at $3–$6 because I could easily lose a hundred dollars in a single session and a hundred bucks is *a whole lot of dough.*" In any event, the question is crucial, and worth thinking about and answering. Obviously you can't play well with scared money, so it's vital that you know where your scared money starts.

"My gulp limit is: _____."

For me, my gulp limit is around $30–$60, and here's why: In order to feel comfortable buying into that game, I have to feel comfortable walking around with a couple grand in my pocket, and carrying that much cash simply makes me antsy. Does this make me a bad person or a weak person? Of course not—I'm just telling the truth about myself to myself. You can do that, can't you? It's easy.

It's easier still if you keep a notebook. I'm not talking about your performance log; we'll get to that later. I'm talking about a private poker journal in which you record useful information from the sessions you play, or discoveries you make, or even ideas from this book that you'd like to have with you and reinforce your memory by writing down.

If you keep such a notebook, then every time I ask you a question like, "What's your gulp limit?" you'll have a place to record and store your answer. If you don't keep such a notebook, you will likely confuse musing about your poker with *really thinking* about your poker. Without a notebook, you're likely to say, in a vague and unfocused way, "I have no gulp limit. I'll play in any game that's good." With a notebook, you're forced to confront yourself directly and concretely. "I really start to sweat at $30–$60. Funny, I used to sweat at $3–$6." Well, change is growth.

So then, what's your gulp limit? Break out a notebook, write down your answer again, and this time tell yourself why. Let it be the start of your poker journal habit, for this habit will pay more dividends than memorizing all the start charts and odds tables in the world. If you keep a notebook, it keeps you honest. I can't put it any more simply than that.

Meanwhile, back in the world of liars, this self-deceptive loser (who keeps no notebook, believe me) has marched himself over to his gulp-limit game and studied it for quite some time. Which, as losers measure time, is about ten sec-

onds. Let's see how many lies he can tell himself before he
even gets into this game.

> That money I lost before doesn't count because it's all just
> a luck game at that limit. Besides, I wasn't warmed up yet,
> not really focused on my play, not like I'm focused now.
> That's right, focused. With this money that I'm taking out
> (of the ATM) now, I will be much more disciplined. It
> should be easy to play well here because, while I don't ex-
> actly have the bankroll to play at this high a limit, I'm
> going to play well and not lose. So I don't really need a big
> bankroll, just a buy-in, or maybe even just a short buy-in.
> Anyway, this lineup doesn't look so tough. So what if
> three players have three racks each? That'll be my
> strength. They're playing super-aggressive, so I'll just wait
> for quality hands and trap them. I'll use their big stacks
> against 'em!

I'll use their big stacks against 'em! That's a funny-looking
lie. It's the one the loser uses when he's really undercapital-
ized for play at his gulp limit, but wants to take a shot with
short money. Sad pathetic loser—*short money equals lost
money*; hasn't he figured that out yet?

The nonsense people think up:

- "One loose call won't kill me."
- "One drink won't hurt my play."
- "One short buy-in is okay."
- "One hour of sleep is sufficient."
- "One more hand and I'll go."

And that's only lies that start with *one*. Can you think
of five lies that start with *two*?

- "Two outs are plenty."
- "Two bets are not too much to defend this blind."
- "Two callers are sufficient for this draw."
- "Two raises in front of me might not mean I'm
  beaten in two places."

- "Two exposed sevens might not mean my pair can't improve."

Can you think of five lies that start with *three*? Try it. Try! This is called *thinking about your game,* and the more honest and articulate you are about your game, the better your game will get.

Look, I don't care if you lie to your friends; I don't care if you lie to your spouse; I don't even care if you lie to me; but you sure as hell better not lie to yourself. If you ask yourself how much you won or lost last night, how long it took you to do it, and why, you'd better have an honest answer, and not only that but a damn detailed one as well! Because this is the simple stuff, Poker Honesty 101, and if you can't get this part right, you have no hope of mastering the rest.

Trouble is, lies are a double-edged sword. Lies come back to bite you. You lie to your enemy when you represent a hand you don't have. That's fine; that's part of the game. Over time, however, you become habituated to lies. You start to think that lying is a good idea. You start to focus on falsehood as something essential to your poker (it is) and thus to your life (it is not).

Here's another one for your notebook, the critical difference between deception and delusion:

> *Deception is what you do to others.*
> *Delusion is what you do to yourself.*

When you've got deception working for you, everyone at the table thinks you're stuck and bleeding, but you know you're not. When you're lost in delusion, however, you think you're still playing well but your foes all know you're on tilt. Where are you then? You're on your way to speaking liarese.

- "I had a run of bad cards."
- "The dealer jinxed me."
- "This one guy just calls with anything. You can't beat a guy like that, unless you play like that."
- "Maybe I should open up my play."
- "An offsuit 9-4 could win, couldn't it? Any two will do, right?"

Is that you? Do you see yourself in all this liarese? If you don't, that's great and I'm happy for you, but if you do (even a little) then you're going to have to work hard to make honesty—self-honesty—the bedrock of your game. Confront yourself and start seeing the truth as it really is. If you want to play Killer Poker, or even just basic winning poker, that's the least you must do. Do it. Do it now. The lie you save may be your own.

LUCK

It is astounding, isn't it, how badly most people play, and how little actual work they do on their game? We should be grateful to them, of course, for their laziness is our profit. When you see the lazy get lucky, however, you start to feel like you're entitled to some of that luck too. After all, someone has to get lucky, right? *Why shouldn't it be you?*

On the other hand, *why should it?*

The Myth of Luck

Luck is for *losers*. Luck is for the unenlightened jerk sitting next to you who thinks that poker is about having the best hand. Luck is for the whimpering simp at the next table who plays to break even. You don't play like that. You're beyond all that.

You don't play to break even. You play to break spines—and you don't do that with luck. You do it with muscle and with raises and re-steal bluffs that allow you to win a pot without having a hand. You do it with bald predation. You do it with the cool, certain knowledge that boldness is the road to poker glory, and that luck won't save the simps when Killer Poker takes control.

The only thing luck has going for it is that it keeps weak players in the game. Remember that when they beat you—by luck—they're really only borrowing the money that will eventually, inevitably, be yours. You don't have to be lucky to win. You don't *want* to be lucky to win. Because luck makes you think you're better than you are, and how can anyone win with that lie floating around in their brain?

Are you lucky? Yes. Unlucky? That too. Here's a truth so essential that I will put it in an important-looking box all by itself:

> *Everyone is exactly as lucky as everyone else.*

Never won the lottery? Me neither, and you know why? It's not because I'm not lucky. It's because I've never played. I know that to five significant figures my chances of winning the lottery are the same—zero—whether I play or not. So I'll never win the lottery—so what? That's not bad luck. That's common sense.

Luck? Yuck!

People change seats for reasons of luck. Don't they know that a seat is only lucky as a function of the butt that's planted in it? Haven't they been told over and over again? And yet they live in ignorance.

I know, I know—sometimes people talk luck to disguise strategy. "This seat is *soooo* unlucky. Guess I'll just move over there to the left of the big raiser." If that's deception it's weak deception. I'm not fooled, and neither are you. In most cases it's the real deal and not strategy anyhow. People who change seats "for luck" are about as capable of higher-level strategic thinking as a patch of lichen is capable of speaking French.

People get mad at me when I get lucky. Like the time I held K♥ Q♥ and the flop came J♥ 2♥ T. The turn was a brick, leaving me with (let's count the outs) eight straight cards, plus seven other flush cards, and six additional shots at an overpair likely to be boss hand if it hit. Twenty-one outs! I hit an out (one of myriad) and won the pot. That's not luck. Hitting an inside straight is luck—moronic luck. The Killer Poker player does without that crutch.

Listen, you're born broke, you die broke; everything else is just fluctuation—and fluctuation *isn't luck*. Fluctuation is the natural, random distribution of outcomes. Call it luck if you want, but don't imagine that yours is any better or worse than anyone else's, because it's not. It's just the same. We're all the same. If you think you're different, you're wrong. Sorry, but you are.

And you're in danger! Your attachment to luck can ruin your game. If you're thinking about luck at all, then you are hooked on outcome, and you can't play Killer Poker if you're hooked on outcome.

You think I'm kidding? You think I'm wrong? Then track this target with me:

You're playing Omaha high-low split, eight-or-better for low—Omaha/8 as it's known. Because you have trouble looking at all four cards at once without flashing them to prying eyes, you peek at them one at a time. That's fine, I have no problem with that. If you have clumsy hands, you take what steps you must to protect yourself. Here's the problem: If the first card is an ace, you immediately start hoping for the second or third or fourth card to be a deuce, so that you can invest heavily in the hand and draw to the nut low, lucky you. Yes, you're hoping to catch lucky—and thus you are hooked on outcome. You're no longer playing the hand you have, but rather the hand you *hope* to have. If that deuce doesn't come, you feel disappointed, unlucky. Then you're at risk for playing the hand even though it's not very playable.

If that deuce *should* come, you're no better off, really, because now you're momentarily high on your own luck. You hoped for an outcome and—*hey, presto!*—you got it. Nothing can stop you now! From this point forward, you feel, somehow, that you deserve favorable outcomes. Having pulled an A-2, you expect to flop a made low. You expect not to be counterfeited or quartered. You expect to get paid off. Why? Because you caught lucky, and that's what lucky players do—they get paid off.

Wrong! Lucky players don't get paid off; they go home broke.

As soon as you think about luck, you're stuck. I know you know it too. Because you're clear-eyed and self-aware, and no slave to superstition. It's just that sometimes you're seduced by luck, because luck is an alluring force. Don't yield! Don't give in!

I've never asked for a deck change in my life. I guess I understand intuitively that the green deck has the same 52 cards as the red deck. Don't you? If you've ever asked for a deck change before, promise yourself that you never will again, except in the rare instance of wanting to *appear* ensorcelled by luck. Instead, do this: Imagine that you're the world's unluckiest person. Mentally prepare yourself for an endless parade of:

- Jack-threes in hold'em.
- Trips in Omaha.
- Start after start of disconnected trash in stud.

- High pairs in lowball.
- Missed flops.
- Brick turns.
- Crippling rivers.

Disconnect from luck. Imagine that it won't be present in your game, won't help you at all, and that the only way you'll ever manage to win is on sheer skill alone.

Because that's the way it truly is—and if people don't know that by now, then I guess they're just unlucky.

> *Even though you've dismissed the issue of luck, never miss an opportunity to brag about how lucky you are. Those who aren't immune to luck may believe you, and misplay against you accordingly.*

FILTERS

In *More Hold'em Excellence: A Winner for Life,* Lou Krieger wrote:

> Some might call me a gambler, but I draw a distinction. A gambler plays even when the odds are immutable and against him. I don't. That's why there is a large coterie of professional poker players, but not a single, solitary, professional roulette or craps player.

Unlike Lou, a lot of people draw no distinction between poker and gambling. This can cause a certain amount of grief to those of us who know and appreciate the distinction because, viewed in a certain light, we poker players look like degenerate gamblers to our friends, family, or disapproving strangers.

Poker qua poker fights this uphill battle in its quest for respectability. So long as poker looks (to the unknowing eye) like the clash of human slot machines, our efforts to make poker be seen and understood as a competition or even a sport seem doomed to failure.

I have explained the difference, many times, only to be met by dull, uncomprehending stares. "Look," I say, "if you could beat Vegas, Vegas wouldn't be there. If you play slots, blackjack, keno, or craps, you're playing against the house and the house can't lose—not in the long run. If you're playing poker, however, you're playing against other players, not the house, and you can make money on the differential between your smarts and theirs."

Like I said, dull, uncomprehending stares. Because if you don't know any better, poker looks like gambling; the two are indistinguishable—if you don't know any better.

Part of me wants to say *who cares?* Who cares if the unwashed multitudes don't understand why I do what I do? Another part of me, however, realizes that their disapproval, even if completely unjustified, can infect my mindset and affect the way I play.

I might pass up a juicy opportunity to play in a tournament with a fat overlay because I don't want to hear someone's "Tsk, tsk, JV's been playing an *awful* lot of poker lately." How is that good for my game?

Of course, if you're playing too much, and playing compulsively, then you do have a gambling problem, but I'm going to assume that you don't. Probably what you have is a people-around-you problem. To solve this problem, you need to put your activity in the proper context so that, at minimum, you don't have to worry about what "your loved ones" think. Have you done this? Have you convinced your mother, father, spouse, friends, kids, coworkers, priest, rabbi, shrink, or dog that poker isn't gambling, and that just because you spend every waking moment working on your game and honing your skills, that doesn't make you a wastrel? Have you? Can you? I think you can. Here's how:

Have your Doubting Thomas or Thomasina flip a quarter, and bet you a quarter on the outcome. (Maybe they won't even bet—some people are just congenitally afraid of a wager. It doesn't make them bad people, but it does make their lives somewhat less colorful than yours and mine.) After you've bet that quarter back and forth a few times, they'll confirm what they already know: that you win about as often as you lose.

Next, offer them the proposition that for every time you win, they pay you a quarter, but for every time they win, you'll pay them 50 cents. Once they start seeing their quarters pile up, explain (if they don't know) that they're now getting 2-1 odds on an even money proposition. This is called having the best of it, and they will now see with their own eyes that they can't lose (not in the long run), and not with this kind of statistical edge.

Now they will also understand the essence of poker as you understand it: positive expectation; getting paid more than the wager is worth, over and over again, for as long as you choose to play. Poker isn't gambling, not when your game is all about seeking, finding, and exploiting that consistent, definable edge. Poker isn't gambling; poker is putting your money in the pot when the reward outweighs the risk—over and over and over again.

Will this argument convince them? Hah! Good luck! (Hah!) It's not that you're not persuasive. It's just that everyone filters reality through their own perceptions. Like the sign says:

> *What you see depends on where you stand.*

If they stand on the (false) assumption that poker is no different from keno, lotto, slots, or the flip-it machine, then, alas, no amount of facts or real evidence will ever make them change their minds. I guess we can live with their disapproval, so long as it doesn't negatively affect our play.

What You See

Like the sign says, "What you see depends on where you stand." Everyone filters reality through perception. Some people do this in a very healthy manner, analyzing available information, weighing it objectively, and using it effectively. Others filter reality through their wants, needs, desires, or fears. Their result is often a skewed version of reality, one that's weak, reactive, hard to trust, and extremely difficult to work with well.

In life, we use filters all the time. If someone runs a red light and totals your car, you process the event through your "what kind of idiot are you?" filter. If you walk away from that bad accident without a scratch, you process the event through your "angels are watching over me" filter.

In poker we use filters all the time too. We filter information through such prisms as past experience, awareness of opponents' tendencies, assumptions about how our opponents view us, and many more. Here are some typical poker filters:

- That guy makes position raises; I've seen him do it before.
- Seat six will defend her blind at all cost.
- I just lost to a suck-out; they'll interpret my raise as a tilt-raise now.
- Seat three has been here all night; he must be tired by now.

What are some poker filters that you use or recognize? Write them down here or in your notebook now.

_____

_____

Precise filters are very powerful. For example, when confronted by a surprise raise from an unexpected source, you can filter this information—the raise—through a specific prism: "Would my opponent be bluffing in this situation? How likely is he to be bluffing now, given that I've rarely seen him raise before?" Processing information through this filter allows you to reach a reasonable conclusion and act accordingly: He's likely to be bluffing only a small fraction of the time, so unless the pot offers extravagant odds, the right thing to do is pass.

It's simple, right? We do it all the time. We do other things all the time, too. They're not so simple and way more nefarious.

Consider the same situation. Someone has raised into you and you're trying to decide whether to call. Instead of filtering information through a useful question like, "How likely is he to be bluffing?" you might filter it through a useless question, even a toxic one, like, "Who does this guy think he is, trying to push me off this pot?" Now, suddenly, your whole basis for evaluation is thrown out of whack because now, suddenly, _you're asking the wrong question!_ You're no longer contemplating how to use certain information effectively, you're contemplating how certain information makes you _feel._ This makes all the difference. Concerned with the question of whether you're being bullied by a bully, you'll call—or even raise—and your action will be an emotional response and not a strategic or tactical response at all.

I'm not singling you out. I'm not calling you bad or flawed. This sort of thinking is very common to the human experience. It's just not very useful in poker.

People use two main filters to deal with information. One is the *process filter, which* asks the question, "How can I use this information to improve my situation?" The other is the *judgment filter, which* asks the question, "How does this information make me feel?" Strong players use their process filter exclusively. They're really only interested in the task of turning available information into correct decisions. Weak players use their judgment filter almost all the time. If they win they feel good. If they lose they feel bad. If they're bluffed out they feel angry. If their blinds are raised they feel resentful. In short, they *feel, feel, feel.* They're obsessed with the question of "How does this information make me feel?"

Theirs is a simple world, though not terribly profitable. Here's why: They have a strong vested interest in feeling *good,* and not *bad,* and they'll act according to this interest, rather than according to sound principles of poker. Their decision-making matrix gets further and further torqued. It's no wonder they can't book a win. They're not just *not* thinking, they're actually *anti-thinking.*

Most people never consciously choose how to process information. They never get free enough in their thinking, or call it enlightened if you want, to see that they have a choice in the matter. They do have a choice, and *you* have a choice, and this decision may be the single most important poker decision you'll ever make. Every hand, every bet, every turn of every card, you have a *choice,* the specific choice of which filter you'll use to deal with the information you've been given. Will you use the information to improve your play, or will you use the information to alter your mood? The former strategy leads to success in Killer

Poker; the latter strategy leads to hopeless weakness and muddy thinking.

So which choice will you make? Will you play poker according to the higher desire to play the best possible game you can? Or would you rather wallow in a fantasyland where every bad thing that happens to you—or even every good thing—is automatically put up on some imaginary scoreboard labeled *How Do I Feel Right Now*?

To me the choice is obvious, but if it's not obvious to you, then consider this: The more you move toward perfect poker, the more you will admire your own willpower, intelligence, strength, and skill. You will, in short, *feel good*. To serve the judgment filter, then, *ignore* the judgment filter. The less attention you pay to the question of how you feel, the better you will play. The better you play, the more admirable you will seem to yourself. The more admirable you seem to yourself, the better you will *feel*—and that's what you wanted all along.

News flash: Nobody's perfect. No one filters information through the process filter all the time. Everyone lets events affect how they feel about themselves. It's inevitable and natural, even human. The question is, what are you gonna do about it? Will you yield to your judgment filter, or will you strive to improve your game?

So now you have new tools to use in your quest for perfect poker. These tools are called "filters," and they allow you to see yourself more clearly—if you choose to. Next time you play poker, bring along your notebook and record every feeling you have during your session. You may feel triumphant when you successfully run a bluff; write that down. You may feel embarrassed when your bluff is busted; write that down, too. Simply record the things you feel, and you'll start to get a sense of how many different *things you feel* in the course of a single day's play. You'll also have a better awareness of where, when, and how your feelings come to dominate your decision making.

For example, have you ever (and don't tell me you haven't because, of course, you have) raised with an inferior hand right after a bad beat? The bad beat made you feel *downcast and forlorn*. It's not the money you're trying to win back quick (though that too). Rather, it's the *good feeling* you had before the bad beat that you're so desperate to re-trieve. "If I can just undo that psychological damage," you think, "then I'll be all right."

Well, you won't be all right, not until you set aside the whole issue of *all right*. Disregard psychological damage and concentrate instead on what you can learn from the beat you just took. Did you misplay the hand? Did your foe? If you misplayed, that's a hole in your game you can fix. If your foe misplayed, that's a hole in his game you can at-tack.

Productive thinking can only take place when you focus on how you play, and not on how you feel.

> *Some of your opponents are absolute slaves to their feelings—and some are not. In your next session, observe your foes and divide them into the categories of* slave *or* free. *You will find that the free foes are the ones most likely to play consistently well.*

EDGE

This idea of dividing your foes into such categories as *slave* and *free* is an easy and generally reliable means of getting a line on their play. You understand this intuitively already, I'm sure: An opponent in obvious misery is an opponent more likely to go on tilt; an opponent more likely to go on tilt is an opponent more likely to lose all his money. The trick is to identify which opponents are in pain—put them in *more* pain—and make sure that they lose all their money to you.

The categorizing needn't stop there. Aggressive and passive, strong and weak, knowledgeable and ignorant—these are all useful ways of dividing, and then conquering, your foes. While it's true that if you try to put everything into a pigeonhole all you will get are a bunch of squished pigeons, it's also true that most poker players run true to form. The good ones are consistently good; the bad ones consistently bad. If you just imagined that each of your foes had a large B(ad) or G(ood) on his or her forehead, you'd have a reliable means of deciding who to attack and who to avoid.

Where Is Your Edge?

Do you have an edge over your foes? Do you play better (stronger, shrewder, more dispassionately, and fearlessly) than they do? Or do they routinely outplay you by forcing you to make decisions that you don't feel comfortable making? If you answer honestly (not filtering your reply through ego or through fear), your response will probably be mixed. There are some players that you can whale on, while others routinely rip you up.

Though some opponents are, in fact, objectively better or objectively worse than you, when it comes to measuring your relative advantage against an opponent, your own state of mind is a critical delimiting factor. Simply put, if you think you have an edge over your foe, you do. If you think he has an edge over you, he does—*and if you're not sure, he has the advantage, too.*

Let's break it down. Suppose there's a foe you know you can beat. How do you go after him? You play strongly and aggressively, and try to put yourself in a situation where your superior skill or decision-making ability is matched against his. In the long run, as you know, you'll both get the same number of good cards and bad cards, but you'll do better with yours because you're playing with the confidence and fierceness required of a winner. For instance, if you know that your opponent has a taste for weak kings, you'll bet the stuffing out of your strong kings and make money on the kicker differential.

If you don't know—really *know*—that you're superior to your opponent, this will affect your play. You'll be more timid and more tentative. You won't push the edges that you have, because you're not sure whether they're real edges or not, and because you're afraid that your potentially superior foe will push back. What's the result? You lose aggressiveness and confidence. You become passive, timid, and reactive. Your play, in short, degrades.

Of course, if you're certain that your opponent is superior to you, then you're just lost going in. You might as well write the guy a check. Why? Because he'll be playing poker at you, but you'll be playing hit-to-win back at him. Fearing that you're outclassed, you'll fall back on the nonstrategy of waiting for good cards and hoping they hold up. Players who need good cards to win *can't* win—not in a strong game.

In a weak game it's a different matter. In many low-limit games, you have to play hit-to-win because the Cally Wallies will call you down, and you have to show the best hand to take the pot. Against strong opponents, though, the thing you fear is not your foes calling you down, but your foes playing back at you, putting you back on your heels. In the presence of this fear, you cannot possibly play your best.

So there are three states of mind: confident, fearful, and

unsure. The only winning state of mind is the confident state of mind, the calm certainty that the opponent you're up against cannot take your money away from you. Obviously this is a consummation devoutly to be wished.

Exactly how are you to achieve the goal? That's easy.

> ***Don't challenge strong players, challenge the weak ones. That's what they're there for.***

If you were up against a bunch of players who you know can destroy you, why in heaven's name would you even give them a chance? Maybe you're trying to prove a point to yourself, about how you can play with the big boys. Maybe your ego won't let you get out of their way. Or maybe, nefariously, you're lying to yourself and saying, "Hell, I'm not scared." If you *are* scared, however, and you know it, just be a man (or woman) and admit it. Drop down a level. Find a softer game. *Go home!* Whatever you do, don't be a chump. Let someone else be the chump for you.

It may be that sheer laziness or inertia blocks you from doing your best in this area. When you go to the club to play poker, do you sign up for all available games within your comfort zone? Do you take the time to watch those games in order to find out which ones are weak? Do you regularly change tables to take advantage of favorable conditions? Or do you just plant yourself in the first available seat and stick it out? The poker universe is chock-full of bad players. You must make sure to face your fair share.

To have a real edge over all your foes, of course, you have to improve your game. Read meaningful poker books. Run simulations. Hone your craft. Record useful thoughts in your notebook. Keep track of your results and study those results to find out where you do and don't excel. In poker, as in almost any line of work, you can't hope to succeed, *really* succeed, unless you're better than 90 percent of the other people trying to do the same thing. *Improve or die.* It's as simple as that.

The third solution, and the most important, is: *Change your state of mind.* Start with the assumption that no one—*no one!*—can beat you when you bring your best game. You may be wrong, and when you're proven wrong, don't be afraid to retreat, but the fact that you believe you're right will give you a significant edge over your opponents who don't know whether they're better than you or not. In other words, the *surer* you are, the bigger edge you have over foes who are *unsure.*

Of course, the vast majority of your opponents don't ever ask themselves whether they're better or worse than anyone else. Most of them wouldn't even know how to phrase the question. They're sleepwalkers, zombies, automated cash machines just waiting for you to come along and punch the code. They simply are not self-aware. Thank heaven for that. People who don't even know themselves can't conceivably know their poker.

So try this thought on for size: *"The only one who can beat me is me."* Repeat it to yourself when you're driving to the club. *"The only one who can beat me is me."* Repeat it when you're sitting down to play. *"The only one who can beat me is me."* Repeat it when you enter your first pot. *"The only one who can beat me is me."* And, most crucially, repeat it to yourself in the heat of combat when things don't go your way. *"The only one who can beat me is me."*

Remember that you are *at risk on every hand.* At risk for playing sloppy. At risk for being inattentive. At risk for letting pride or fear turn you away from the path of perfect poker. At risk for turning a bad beat into a major tilt, and at risk for sheer *stupidity.* Constantly guard against these risks. Constantly monitor your own state of mind. If you are *confident* and *concentrating,* then you're in great shape, but if you've become fearful or wishful, or even uncertain or inattentive, your game has taken a turn for the worse. You've lost your edge. You need to get fixed or get out.

The only one who can beat you is you.

You know it's true. You see the evidence of it every time you play. When you play monkey poker, you get crushed, but when you play Killer Poker, when you bring all your fearlessness and focus and skill to bear, then you are unstoppable.

The only one who can beat you is you. Now the only question is this: Are you going to let that happen?

Of course not. You wouldn't be a Killer Poker player if you did.

This may strike you as strange, but the next time you play poker, try to change tables as often as possible. Use this exercise to train yourself into a flexible, mobile frame of mind. A good player moves quickly to avoid peril or to seize opportunity.

How to Gain an Edge

The only one who can beat you is you. That's a useful tidbit, but it's awfully general, and thus not ultimately helpful to our cause. To change bad habits, you need to understand where, when, and exactly how you beat you. Do you make pointless bets? Retreat in the face of raises? Tilt away the end of your rack? Do you let other players' scare tactics put you off your game? What, in other words, are the precise holes in your play? I've already told you to keep a poker journal. Within that notebook I would expect to see a comprehensive and growing list of all the ways that you beat you.

Will that be a problem for you? Will you find it awkward, difficult, or even humiliating to confess to yourself that you stubbornly play low pairs in seven stud in the face of two raises by rocks? I should think that the emotional pain of this searching inventory would hurt you less than the material pain of leaking money out of your wallet through the holes in your play, but you decide for yourself. All I can tell you is that the more you get used to facing your flaws, the less noxious and frightening they become.

Below you'll find an excerpt from my flaws notebook, and if I tell you that I've solved all these problems you have my permission to call me a liar to my face. Nobody fixes *all* his or her poker problems—not you, not me, not the next poker champion of the world. The best we can anticipate is to move along a continuum toward better and better play. Perfection is an unattainable ideal. If anyone tells you he plays perfect poker, you have my permission to call him a liar to his face.

While it's fine to be confident in your ability, I think it's better to be confident in your honesty. Rather than boasting, "I never miss a bet," say (and think) instead, "I try to stay on top of every situation so that I can use my awareness and my skills to extract maximum value." That's power poker—Killer Poker—but it's also humble poker and honest poker . . . a hidden strength of your game.

So then, speaking as someone who does not play perfectly, but does strive to move down the path every day toward that goal, let me say this about how I defeat my own best intentions at the table:

- I become bored when I'm not involved in the hand.
- I allow distractions to turn my attention away from the game.
- I let other players get inside my head.

- I play hunches.
- I have a terrible memory.
- I spend my bankroll.
- I get affronted at the table when someone calls me stupid to my face.
- If I play long enough, I enter this sort of fugue state where my thinking becomes hazy, and bad decisions start to look like good ones.
- I get feral as I approach the end of my rack.
- I still measure the success or failure of a session by whether I ran red or black, and not by whether I played well. When will I get over *that?*

All I'm trying to do with this information is be honest with myself. The fact that I'm being honest with you as well—well, perhaps this lets you see that it's possible to be honest (with yourself and with others) about your poker flaws and not have to experience ego death. So go ahead and start that flaws list now. It's a list you'll revisit again and again as the refinement of your game continues.

EXCESS

Greed, hubris, and fear: These three words can comprise a sentence of death for the Killer Poker player, for they represent three specific ways that good players routinely defeat their own best interests.

I'm sure you know these words, but let's recapitulate just the same:

Greed   Excessive, inordinate, or rapacious desire, especially for wealth

Fear   Excessive apprehension, consternation, terror, horror, or fright

Hubris   Excessive pride, self-satisfaction, egoism, or conceit

Note that the common denominator in these definitions is the word *excessive*. Note and be warned, for excessive *anything* is bad for you (at least in poker if not in sex).

So. Let's look at greed. "Greed is good," said Gordon Gekko in the movie *Wall Street*, and who are we to argue with Gekko, or with pop visionary Oliver Stone who put those words in Michael Douglas's mouth? Still, I sound a cautionary bell because excessive greed is not good, not in poker. Even the seemingly invincible Gekko went down, and it was greed that brought him low.

The trouble with greed is the massive trouble greed gets you into. One bet at a time, two bets, or three—greed can drive you crazy and broke if you let it control your play.

Consider this: You're playing against a total weakie, and it's surely only a matter of time before he shipwrecks himself upon the rocky shoals of your superior play. All you have to do is wait for his own weak mistakes to mow him down—but you don't want to wait. You want his money and you want it now. Greed makes you rash, and greed makes you rush. Greed makes you press thin edges or possibly nonexistent ones. Next thing you know, your unworthy opponent has taken advantage of your inappropriate play-making, caught lucky, and gone home with your dough, alas.

Most working pros hope for a minimum earn rate of one big bet an hour—possibly the very extra bet that you, in your haste, have been trying to squeeze out of unprofitable situations. Relax. Take a breath. Successful poker is not a get-rich-quick scheme. You're in this for the long haul. You can be greedy, but you have to be patient too.

Superior play wins money, but greed defeats superior play like a cat defeats tinfoil and tinfoil defeats a microwave. Resist greed. Paradoxically the more you resist greed, the more money you will win and the more satisfied your need for greed will be. Why? Because poker played greed-free is steady, solid, well-considered poker—winning poker, in short. So practice patience. Those chips will make their way to your stack eventually. Remember:

> *You just need to win; you don't need to win right now.*

Here's an example of greed bringing a stud player low: Playing seven-card stud, you have two pair going into seventh street. Your foe across the table has apparently been chasing a flush, and you can't discern from his tells whether his last card helped him or not. Maybe he hasn't even looked.

It's up to you to check or bet. Greed says *bet! Bet and get those extra chips!* But there's a problem with this thinking. If he missed his flush, he can't call you, and if he made his flush, he'll raise you back. We often overlook this sad reality because the strength of our hand, plus the lure of greed, blinds us to the simple truth that the only hands that can call us are hands that can beat us. Next thing we know, we're facing a raise and looking at a hard decision. Do we want to waste an extra bet just to find out what we already know? No. In all instances, let your read on your opponents, not your own greed, guide your play.

Now let's look at fear. Fear, in certain circumstances, is a healthy quality. Fear keeps us from sleeping with spouses not our own or sticking our heads out of trenches. Reasonable fear—folks call it caution—keeps us on our toes. Excessive fear, however, provokes weakness and errors, and Killer Poker wants no part of that.

Consider: You take A♥ J♣ into a flop of J-8-3 with one heart. You bet the flop, as you should, and thin the field to a single caller, a player you know to be reasonable and sensible. The turn is a second heart. Putting your opponent on a straight draw or a jack with an okay kicker or an 8 with an ace, you bet, as you should, and get called. The river is a baby heart and suddenly you're scared. So then you do something dumb: You check. The fear that your foe caught a runner-runner flush caused you to *check*. Where did that nonsense move come from? Remember that this is a reasonable, sensible player. He's most likely not in the hand on the strength of a non-nut backdoor flush draw—in fact you already put him on other holdings. Here in the moment, fear makes you give him too much credit for a hand he doesn't have. Fear makes you miss a bet.

Where greed makes you bet too much, fear makes you bet too little. Neither place is where you want to be. Note that in both cases, your thinking is dominated not by analysis of the situation but by animal response to emotion. This is why we work so hard to filter information through process and not judgment; for the sake of seeing things as they are and not as we hope, or alternately fear, them to be.

You're in the small blind with K-Q, and someone in late position raises into you. You know this player to be an opportunist out to steal your blind, so you raise him back. That's good; that's plenty fearless. But then he raises *you* back, and suddenly you hit the brakes. You call and await the flop with trepidation. The flop comes K-x-x. You bet—he raises, putting you back on your heels once again. You can practically see the A-K in your opponent's hand. But wait! Didn't you say he was a mighty blind stealer? Then what makes you think he's got A-K? Fear, that's what. Fear. You're afraid that the hand that *could* beat you *will* beat you, and it causes you to slow down your betting or even (horrors!) throw your hand away.

That's no way to win money. You have to swallow your

fear and *fight back!* Otherwise, you might as well just hand them your wallet at the door.

Base your decision on the likeliest scenario, not the worst-case one. "Fear," to quote Frank Herbert's *Dune*, "is the mind killer." Don't let it kill yours.

Now we come to hubris, and hubris is worse than greed and fear put together. Why? Because evil hubris is so close to its good cousins confidence and arrogance that it's hard to tell where they leave off and it kicks in.

Here's confidence: You look around the table and see a lot of familiar faces. You've jousted with this crew and bested them before. Available empirical evidence, plus your meticulous and detailed records, suggests that you can kick their individual and collective posteriors. With confidence, and maybe even arrogance, you proceed to do just that.

Now here's hubris: You look around the table and see a lot of unfamiliar faces. Not having observed anyone's play for any reasonable length of time, you unreasonably conclude that you can best them all, on the strength of your innate poker skill and cagey plays. So you throw on the headphones and don't even bother to look for tells. That's how good you think you are. Know what? You may be right, but then again you may be wrong. You won't know for sure if you don't study your foes closely and see them clearly, two things that hubris will prevent you from doing. Seen through the gauze of hubris, all foes seem weak. But not all foes *are* weak, and there's the lurking danger.

What's that thing pride goeth before? Oh yeah, a fall.

Hubris in action: You're playing $1–$5 seven-card stud, a real bottom-feeder's game, while you wait for a seat in the hold'em game you crave. You assume, without evidence, that all of your opponents are squishy-brained tourists with no loftier ambition, nor likelier fate, than to go broke slowly. On your first hand, you pick up split kings and drive that sucker pair for all it's worth. One old lady calls along, and you figure her for a foolish optimist, because isn't that what all poker-playing old ladies are supposed to be? You're fearless (good) but also reckless (bad) and inattentive (worse!). Did you not notice how her eyes lit up when she paired her door card? Why do you assume that she doesn't have trips? Because she's a little old lady, and little old ladies never have trips?

What's that thing pride goeth before?

She calls you down through sixth street, then raises on seventh street into your unimproved pair. She takes down a pot that you *shamelessly* overplayed. It's a good thing that they've called you to your hold'em seat now, because this little stud game you thought you could run over is about to run over you. It's also a bad thing that they've called you to your hold'em seat, however, because you're already half-way tilty and you haven't even gotten into your game of choice.

Pride made you do that: hubris. You burdened yourself with the assumption that you're better than they are. That's trouble. The kind of trouble you don't need.

> *Show respect for every game you're in—whether you think the game deserves it or not.*

So there you have them: greed, fear and hubris, just waiting to strike you down. Each is reasonable in reasonable circumstances, but ruinous in excess. In all events, always track the underlying motivation for the moves you make.

- Do you see a reasonable opportunity to punish a weak opponent, or are you just in a big fat hurry to bully someone's money away?

- Do you follow through with appropriate aggression, or does something make you flinch in the face of (perceived, not real) danger?
- Do you credit your opponents with the abilities they have, or do you imagine them to be houses of wood or straw to the big bad wolf that is you?

Once you've tracked your findings, record them. Write them down, so that you can remind yourself how greed, fear, and hubris can leech into your game and suck your money away.

> *Most players fear a check-raise on the turn more than any other bet in hold'em. Why? Because the check-raiser is demonstrating a willingness to invest two big bets—at least twice as much as he's invested in an unraised pot to this point. So if you see opponents who veer toward fear, check-raise them on the turn a little more frequently and put their own fear to work against them.*

Subdivide and Conquer

In my book *Creativity Rules! A Writer's Workbook*, I make the point that writers and other creative types often find themselves confronted by problems that, as presented, are too large or too complex to solve all at once. In order to be worked effectively, these problems must be broken down into their component parts—successively smaller and smaller problems—until they are finally reduced to something manageable: a problem one can actually solve.

I take this same subdivide-and-conquer approach to poker, and you see an example of this in my analysis of greed, fear, and hubris. It's not enough to know that there are negative forces at work in my game or your game. To know these forces well, we have to give them names—names like greed, fear, and hubris—and in this way we make it possible to examine each of them in turn and study the impact they have on our play. It's never useful, in other words, to say, "I suck, my poker sucks," unless we can cite specifically where, when, and how our poker sucks.

You might say, "Well, that's no fun. Who wants to admit that their poker sucks?" But if you embrace the fact of your flaws on the level of creative problem solving, then the exploration of your flaws can, in fact, be fun. Simply say to yourself, "Okay, given that my game does suck, can I put my finger on just one specific way in which my performance lets me down? Oh, yeah, here's one: I forget to look downstream for tells. Okay, next time I play, I'll try to do better with that." That's a challenge you can meet; that's a problem you can solve.

What this process does is take a messy and unproductive amorphous mass of self-loathing ("I suck, my poker sucks") and turns it into a detailed and specific piece of poker awareness ("I forget to look for tells"). What was toxic negativity is now useful self-knowledge. What was cause for pessimism is now cause for optimism. It may be a small thing, this distinction between "I'm bad" and "I'm improving," but it makes a big difference.

The whole point of poker introspection is not to bring yourself down but to raise yourself up. You can only improve if you first identify where you need to improve, and you can only identify that need if you get past denying that the need exists. That's why we say that no one plays perfect poker: Because if you imagine for a moment that your play is perfect, you deny the need to improve. Then growth and learning grind to a halt. Who wants that?

So in the name of subdivide-and-conquer, we constantly look for new and different ways to examine our game. Herewith, then, the Seven Deadly Sins, as viewed through a poker prism.

SINS

Sins. According to Pope Gregory the Great and St. Thomas Aquinas and others, there are seven deadly ones. Let's apply them to poker and see how they hurt your game.

Pride

The excessive belief in one's own abilities or entitlements can inject all sorts of chaos into an otherwise orderly playing universe. Those guilty of this sin will play in games too tough to beat and suffer the general unhappy consequences of that bad choice. They will also make situational mistakes by (mis)reasoning that they can outplay certain opponents after the flop in hold'em or Omaha, or on later streets in stud, forgetting that their opponents may be so ignorant or inattentive that there's no such thing as outplaying them at all. The solution to this sin is this: Stay within yourself and stay humble. This will keep pride from taking you for a ride.

Envy

Do you look at the big winners in the big games and say, "Geez, what have they got that I haven't got?" They've got skill (maybe), dedication to the game (probably), and chips and money (for sure). If all you have is the yearning desire to be like the big boys, then you're a victim of envy. You will remain a victim until you wed your desire for lofty heights to the hard work that attaining such heights requires. Anyone can envy, but precious few can improve.

Gluttony

Anything that's worth doing is worth overdoing, right? If you've played a five-hour session, why not try for nine? Forgetting for a moment that your desire to play poker was well sated after the third hour, you must know that playing beyond the limits of your stamina is an invitation to a nightmare. Play till you've had enough *and then quit!* The game will still be there tomorrow, and your appetite for it will still be there, too. Gluttony equals eating; be careful lest you eat yourself.

Lust

Although people commonly think of lust in terms of sex, lust is defined as an inordinate craving or desire for the pleasures of the body. All pleasures, not just sex. If you use drugs, that's lust. If you drink alcohol while you play poker, that's lust too. One might even say that sports betting is lust, since what many of us crave when we bet is not the financial payback but the *body thrill* of our bet coming through. None of these things, of course, abet your best poker effort. Be a Buddhist when you play poker: Disconnect from lust and let the rewards that are due you come to you.

Anger

Anger, so they say, is manifested in the individual who spurns love and opts instead for fury. Well, where are you with this one? Do you have love when you play—love for your fellow man and woman, even the dealer? Or do you find yourself raging against the unfair and arbitrary forces of (what you perceive as) blind luck and stupidity that surround you? Anger is a red cloud of poison gas that obscures your vision and occludes your common sense. It's death to play angry. Get calm or get out.

Covetousness

This is the desire for material wealth or gain. Covetousness exists in an individual who is ignoring the realm of the spiritual. Where do you stand on that? Do you put your poker play (and your life) in the context of higher forces? I'm not telling you to believe in God, but I am telling you to believe in *something*. It will make your life rise and keep covetousness at bay.

Sloth

Sloth is the avoidance of work. Sloth is where you cease reading, studying, or thinking about your game in the mistaken belief that you've somehow *got it licked.* Trust me, you don't have it licked, if for no other reason than that you're constantly in dynamic struggle with real opponents in the real world. If they're denying sloth—if they're working hard to be better players every day—then they're moving ahead of you in this race. In the face of fierce competition, if you're not steadily getting better, you're steadily getting worse.

Sin Scenarios

People don't talk a lot about sin these days. It has become unfashionable to use such a spiritually charged word in polite (secular) society. When I raise the subject I'm not concerned with sin as it relates to heaven or hell, except the specific heavens and hells that we encounter every day at the poker table. Nor am I, believe me, trying to guide you down any path toward (my own subjective version of) righteousness. I don't care about sin, per se. I'm just trying to improve your game and mine.

With that in mind, let's search together for specific situations in which we commit these play-degrading sins. I'm not afraid to go first.

Pride "I tangle with tough players and put myself into needless (and expensive) confrontations with trickier, more knowledgeable and more fearless foes."	

Envy "When I look around the table and see other players with stacks of racks, I feel an urgent need to win as much as they've won—*right freaking now!*" When envy rushes in, patience fades away.	

Gluttony "Sometimes I play poker even when I don't want to play poker. I even battle traffic and a long drive just because I feel a thirst to play."	

Lust "Man what it *feels* like to rake in a big pot. Forget about outplaying my opponents; just the visceral kick of scooping and stacking and racking all those chips. It's a buzz, pure and simple, a buzz."	

Anger "I'm most likely to direct my anger at myself: *You dolt! How could you make that play? What the <u>hell</u> were you thinking?*" Inner-aimed anger is no less harmful than outer-aimed anger.	

Covetousness "If I had more money, I'd be happier. If I were happier, I'd be more relaxed. If I were more relaxed, I'd play better poker. If I played better poker, I'd have more money." What kind of trap is that?	

Sloth "I used to think about my sessions and *really plan them* while I drove to the card room. I seem to have left that habit behind, as if I already know what I'm going to do in any situation I'm likely to encounter." So what if I do? Don't I still have something to learn?	

Now you take a stab at it, either here or in your notebook:

Pride	
Envy	
Gluttony	
Lust	
Anger	
Covetousness	
Sloth	

If you resist this sort of exercise—if it strikes you as a Communist study cell exercise in conspicuous confession—I can certainly relate to your resistance. Look, you don't have to go public with this information. You can keep it safely tucked inside your own introspection. I suspect that you have these feelings about your play anyway. You may just not have used grids like these to parse and clarify your thoughts. It's a hard thing, yes, but not so hard (or anyway not so costly) as making moves at the table driven by sloth, covetousness, or pride, rather than by common sense and good play.

How do you feel when you rake a big pot? What specific **mind** *and* **body** *reactions can you identify? Do these reactions make you more or less likely to participate in the very next hand? Does* **playing a rush** *amount to* **chasing the buzz** *for you?*

You know what? This whole business of sin may be just too emotionally charged to deal with. After all, poker is intended to be a vocation at best, an avocation at worst. It's not intended to be a spiritual passage to a higher place (although there are times . . .). So let's just dial things back from the sacred to the mundane, shall we? The preachers and the pious may speak of sins, but here in the postmodern world, more and more people speak of bugs—errors in the software. In the next chapter we'll examine ourselves and our play through that prism, and see what happens when we dedicate ourselves to finding, and annihilating, the bugs that infest our play.

2

♣♠♦♥

FIXING THE HOLES

♣♤◇♡

BUGS

When a computer program has flaws and doesn't run properly, we call those flaws "bugs." Poker players have bugs in their game and the harder they work at fixing their bugs, the cleaner, more efficient, and ultimately more profitable their play becomes.

It's easy to fix bugs in computer programs because the standard of measurement is fairly cut-and-dried: Either the program runs properly or it doesn't. It's not so easy in poker, where everything is variables, angles, percentages—the infamous "it depends" of poker. Plus in software there's no emotional risk: Just because the program is flawed doesn't mean that the programmer is also flawed. Fixing bugs in your poker game requires flexible thinking, a willingness to learn, humility, and a clear-eyed appraisal of your own strengths and weaknesses.

Whew! That's quite a lot. On a practical and emotional level, it's quite a lot. It's also quite simple. In fact it's a fact:

> *If you want to improve your play, you have to squash your bugs.*

46

We've already examined our game in terms of sins—a global view, if you will, of the way we play. In this section we'll take a closer look at our bugs, the small-but-costly (or not so small and even more costly) errors that affect the smooth running of our system. You have a notebook. Record some bugs that have bugged you in the past. For instance, perhaps you have fallen victim to these:

- I carelessly fritter away the last few chips in my rack.
- I give up in tournaments when I become short-stacked.
- I defend my blinds too much.
- I criticize the play of other players.
- I check and call too much.
- I play too many hands.
- I overvalue suited cards.
- I play more aggressively when I feel I'm "due."
- I raise when I haven't raised in a while, just because I feel antsy.

Or these:

- _____
- _____
- _____
- _____
- _____
- _____
- _____
- _____
- _____

If you find it hard to look honestly at your bugs, get someone else to look at them for you. In the software business, these bug hunters are called *beta testers*, and it's their specific job to identify what's wrong and what doesn't work. Just as this beta testing is vital to the ultimate success of the software, a dispassionate examination of your play is vital to the continued growth, health, and profitability of your game. What you want is a knowledgeable colleague or friend who can watch your play for a session or two or three and report back to you on what he finds.

Some of the bugs they discover may astound you. Consider the case of Joel's card protector.

Like many of us, Joel uses a token—in Joel's case a little porcelain duck—to cover his cards and protect them from accidentally being fouled or swept into the muck. Whenever he's dealt a hand, he'll peek at his cards and then immediately cover them with his duck. Or so he thinks. Imagine his surprise when his beta tester informs him that he only protects the hands he intends to play. Otherwise he holds the cards between his fingers, ready to muck in turn, as if the act of protecting bad hands is more trouble than it's worth.

How would you exploit that tell? You'd look at Joel before you bet. If you saw his cards under his card protector, you'd know he had value. If he had them in hand, you could bet or raise with impunity, knowing that he had already given up on the cards. How much money do you think you could take off him in the long run with a tell as big as that?

> *Always handle your hole cards in exactly the same manner, whether you intend to play them or not.*

A beta tester, or bug collector, then, is there for your own protection—if your ego and pride can stand what this person has to say:

- You flash your cards to the player on your left.
- You check-raise all your draws on the flop.
- You play rags on a whim.
- You draw to long shots when you don't have odds for a call.
- You overplay middle pairs.
- You chase too much.
- You bluff too much.
- You don't pay attention to the play of hands you're not in.
- You loosen up when you're running badly.

Some call this sort of exercise *assisted self-discovery*. Others call it *a fair working definition of hell*. But if you can stand to have someone recite such an ugly litany of your play, and then take that information and put it to work, your game will improve by quantum degrees. I guarantee it. Why? Because bad news leads to good play. It's axiomatic. You can't fix your bugs if you don't know they're there, but simple awareness that a problem exists takes you most of the distance toward repairing it.

Chase too much? *Tell yourself you do!* Now you know. Now you can dial back on your chasing. Can you honestly stand not to be that minimally honest with yourself about your poker play? I think you can. So what if it hurts to hear the cold, hard truth? Doesn't it hurt more to lose money?

There are ego issues all over poker. If you allow yourself to admit that you don't know something, or don't do something properly, your ego naturally feels threatened. Hasn't your ego figured out yet that *winning* is the best ego-stroke of all? Put your ego aside! Challenge your intellect to play the best that you can. Then, when your game improves and *you win,* your ego and your wallet both get to feel good about what you've done.

Do you still feel threatened by criticism or self-criticism? All I can tell you is grow up or get out. Poker's no place for the weak, and defense of ego is weak by definition. Plus there's this: You'll find that it's much easier to see the bugs in other people's play once you've become honest about the bugs in your own.

Why? Because pretty much everyone thinks pretty much the same way about poker. So pretty much everything you're thinking (especially at a poker table but also everywhere else) is pretty much what everyone else is thinking, too. This, then, is the secret of mind reading: To read their minds, just read your own. If you're frank and honest in your appraisal of your bugs, you can reliably predict and identify the presence of those very same bugs in others.

Consider this scenario: Between yourself and your beta tester, you have discovered that you're likely to play any trashy hand right after a bad beat because you want the luck to "even out" immediately. You have ceased this nonsense, so you now look around to see who else has that bug. There! Seat one! He's got it! He *hates* the bad beat! He *needs* to get well right away. Raise into him with impunity. He's got the disease you just got over. He'll call with a bad hand for the sake of salving the wound. You *know* he will, because you used to, too.

Here, then, is a simple three-step process for using *your own flaws* against your foes:

1. Discover them in yourself.
2. Detect them in others.
3. *Attack!*

Do you stubbornly cling to kings when there's an ace on the flop? That's a bug! Stomp it out! *Then see who else does it, and punish them when you can!*

Killer Poker is demanding, sure: It requires a level of honesty you may not entirely be comfortable with yet. On the other hand, it's really not so tough. In the end it's as simple as looking in a mirror—although maybe one covered with bugs.

> *We've talked about recruiting a poker pal to beta test your game, but to this point that's all it's been—just talk. Don't go forward in this book or in your game until you've actually had someone **look over your shoulder** while you play. Then return the favor. You can also learn a lot about your own bugs by studying the bugs of your buddies.*

GHOSTING

There is a risk, of course, in projecting your bugs onto other players. That risk is called "subject-object confusion." In this state of mind, you come to assume that all your foes have all your bad habits. This may or may not be the case. They may, in fact, be much healthier in their play—or, alternatively, much more direly afflicted—than you. Nevertheless, it is a useful exercise to blur the distinction between the way you play and the way your opponents come at you. This is how you get inside their minds. This is how you predict their behavior. This is how you come to know what they're holding as clearly as if their cards were face up on the table. It's a technique I call *ghosting*.

This isn't just a matter of watching other people play;

rather, it's crawling inside their minds and playing along with them. Once you've folded, identify the lead player in the hand and let yourself see the hand from his point of view. Start by determining what you think he has (always prepared to update your evaluation based on later actions) and then play along, asking yourself what you would do with those cards in that situation.

This is an easy way to discover who makes what kind of mistakes. Suppose you're ghosting a player who attacks a dangerous flop (say K♠ Q♠ x) very aggressively. You might predict that he has a legitimate holding—a real hand or a real draw—because that's what you'd have in that situation. When you discover that he's been doing all this attacking with something like a pair of eights, you've learned something crucial about his play: He gets out of line. When he next bets into you, you can assign a certain probability that he's out ahead of his hand again.

Eventually, when you get good at this, you can ghost all active participants in a hand at the same time. Your inner monologue would sound something like this:

> Okay, three players are in the hand and the flop gives us a flush draw. Seat three's check-raise indicates that seat three has that draw. Flat-calls of the raise from seats six and eight reveal that neither is superstrong. Now the turn is a little brick. Seat six bets, probably with top pair, good kicker. Whoops, now here comes a raise from seat eight. What does that mean? Did he call with an underpair and hit trips on the turn? I've seen him do it before. So okay, seat eight has a set, seat six has top pair, and seat three's still on a draw. The river's a brick. I predict check, check, bet, fold, and a crying call. Yup, that's what happened. Seat six had top pair, eight had trips, and I ghosted the hand correctly.

This sort of activity pays dividends on so many levels. First, of course, it gives you clues to your opponents' tendencies: what their calling requirements are; whether they chase with bad odds; when they can be moved off a hand. Second, it keeps you mentally involved in the game. You don't have time to let your mind wander if you assign yourself the task of ghosting every hand you're not in. Third, it prepares you for the crucial task of ghosting hands you *are* in. The more practiced you are at getting inside your foes' heads when you're not holding cards, the easier it becomes to do so when you are.

In the following section you'll find an even more detailed exercise in ghosting a hand. It's an exercise I encourage you to try for yourself. You may feel that this sort of activity is beyond you, since it seems to be "writing," an "act of creation," but it's not creation, it's merely recording what happened. You can do that, can't you? Record what's right in front of your face? The fun part is imagining the reasoning and rationalizations behind the actions. This is good for your game: It deepens your knowledge of the way people think. So take out your notebook (if you dare) and take the time (if you dare) to transcribe fully and completely the play of a hand you've observed, or participated in—or even just imagined.

A Ghosting Scenario

If you don't think it's a problem, then it's not, but I watched you play that hand, and brother you've got a problem. K-9 unsuited? Land o' Goshen, what were you thinking? You limped in in early position and ended up taking a five-way flop for four bets. *Four bets!* What flop could you possibly have loved with that hand? Q-J-T? It leaves you vulnerable to the A-K, which is very likely out there in any five-way four-bet scenario. Or maybe you'd like a set of nines. Even then you could easily be looking at A-9, couldn't you? After all, A-9 is less swilly than the K-9 you played. Okay, so then you're dreaming of flopping a full house, and while I admire your optimism, if that's the kind of poker you play, then you've got bigger problems than I thought.

But that's not even what happened. It's not even close. Here's what really happened. You got dealt your K-9 and decided you'd play a little Killer Poker by popping the pot in early position. That's fine, I don't have any problem with that—if you see it through. At the last minute, though, you noticed someone downstream loading a reraise—filling his hand with chips—so you chickened out. But, oops, you forgot to fold and you just called, and that's where you got trapped in the hand.

And the raiser behind you? He just called! It was the old fake-load and you fell for it. Two other calls and now it's back to the big blind, who raises, and she can't be raising with nothing, not into that crowd. She's trying to build the pot, not thin the field. You know this—you *know* you do!

Instead of making a strategic escape, you look at that burgeoning pot and start computing the odds of your straight draw, forgetting for a moment that you don't have a draw, really, but only pieces of one. If that doesn't work, you'll predict the flopping of two pair. Anything to delude yourself into calling, which you do. You don't have odds; you don't have outs; and you don't have expectations. You don't have anything except the sad rationale that any hand worth one bet is worth two.

Now the fellow behind you gets frisky. That fake raiser? He decides he likes his hand well enough to want to see this pot capped before the flop, and he figures that the big blind will oblige him if he puts in a raise right here. Sure enough that happens, and the action comes back to you. You use whatever justifications you didn't use before (*good money after bad* usually works here) to get yourself to call. "Look at the size of that pot! Man, this is *action!*"

As we've already discussed, you hate almost any flop you hit here. (Okay, I'll give you quads.) You, alas, have elevated creative wishful thinking to a high art, so let's see how you screwed this particular pooch further still.

The big blind had a real hand; her actions proved it. So did the frisky raiser behind you. So even if the other callers are (like you) present in error, you know that there are at least two hands out there that are better than yours, and you know exactly where they are. Yet you choose to ignore this useful information. Why? Because the flop comes 9-6-3 rainbow, so now you have top pair, big kicker, and who throws away that hand, right?

Killer Poker says *raise,* right? Yes, yes, yes, raise, raise, raise, but please, please, please not into this thicket.

A-K or A-Q won't fold, and their overcards give them odds to call, for they have six presumptive outs out of 47 cards—7-1 against—with 20 bets already in the pot. You know a big pair won't fold, nor would any of the three possible open-ended straight draws (8-7, 7-5, 5-4). (Don't bother discounting these draws; if you're goofy enough to be here for four bets, so is the boho holding 8-7 suited.) Maybe your bet will drop a gutshot draw or a middle pair, but that's about all.

So a bet in this situation would have almost no power to move people off the pot, yet when the big blind checks, you bet, because, hey, *carpe collectum,* right? Seize the pot, right? Right?

Yes, right.

Or more precisely, *wrong.*

You don't bet here. You have no business being here in the first place but in any case, look around! Didn't the big blind raise before the flop? Twice? Didn't you put her on a big pair? Wouldn't a big pair love to make a check-raise now? And you gave her a shot.

Well, the bet goes around. The frisky fake-loader behind you just calls. The other two fold, but the big blind (yes) check-raises. Now you're starting to suffer because it finally dawns on you that you'll have to hit to win here. So you just call, but Frisky reraises. You hope (and therefore believe) that it's a foreclosure raise, made by a draw looking for a free card on the turn, but what kind of hand could he have reraised with pre-flop that's turned into a decent draw now? Besides, could he really hope to slow the big blind down? She hasn't been slow this whole hand.

Of course she reraises and of course you, with top pair and big kicker, call both bets because suddenly you decide that they're both lying sacks and they're trying to steal your pot—*your pot!*—and you will *not* have *that*!

The Elvis of your rationality has left the building of your brain. Now we'll have a moment of silence while you pray for a card.

You pray for a nine or a king. Lo and behold your prayer is answered! The board now reads 9-6-3-K with no threatening suit noise to distract you from the warm and fuzzy feeling you have that your bleak K-9 has just developed some serious stealth potential. You try to imagine the hands that could be out against you. You discount all legitimate hands and see instead a lot of 8-7s and 5-4s who will fold weeping when the board bricks their straight draw on the river.

So naturally when the big blind checks, you bet. Mr. Frisky raises because his A-K likes that king a lot, especially if he puts you on A-9. Whoops, now the big blind reraises (another check-raise!) and now you just call because what if she really does have kings? Then Frisky fires back and you're whipsawed but good. What a mess.

By now you're pretty far gone, so far deep into delusion that a three on the river actually excites you. You don't see how that card can hurt you, because who'd be in the midst of this firestorm with a naked three? The big blind bets out. You swallow hard. You feel you must be beaten, but you call just the same, just for the size of the pot. Mr. Frisky mutters something like "Well, if you can call I can't," and throws away his hand, saving himself the final big bet that you just wasted.

So, what does the big blind have? Well, what's a raising hand for a big blind? Let's all say it together, shall we? *Pocket aces!*

Yes, the big blind had pocket aces all along—pocket aces elevated to the status of winning hand by a nondescript pair-card on the river. The big blind had aces, and she played them exactly as you'd expect aces to play. The big blind had aces, an obvious reality you ignored every step of the way. The big blind had aces, and you impaled yourself on them. Why did you do that? Because desire vetoed common sense, to the tune of exactly 18 small bets, and this is the mistake you make every time. You let reality be colored by your need to win, and as long as you keep doing that, you will keep losing money. You don't stand a ghost of a chance.

And I know, because I'm the ghost inside your head.

> *In hold'em, the odds of starting with a pair or an A-x are 4-1 against. This means that in any full game, an average of two players will have a real hand on each deal. So the next time you're tempted to mix it up with crummy cards, remember that you're probably beaten in two places going in.*

The Ghost Inside Your Head

Good players review their own play, good or bad. They ghost inside their own minds, as it were, constantly examining and appraising the decisions they make and the motivation that underlies those choices. Sometimes the news isn't good. Sometimes they have to look back on a session or a hand (or a month or a year) and admit to themselves what utter dunderheads they were back there.

Well, the past is the past. This is no time for recrimination, but it is time for—here's our theme again—a fearless and searching appraisal of your play. Just as you can learn a lot about your opponents by ghosting and recording what they do, you can learn a lot about yourself by recording what *you* do.

I'm a writer, okay? I am. I like to write. So it shouldn't surprise anyone to discover that I'm willing to take the time to recount on paper an episode or two that I've had at the table. So you're not a writer—so what? You can still recall and record what happened, can't you? But you'll only do this if you consider the reward great enough. I think that the reward is considerable, and I urge you to demonstrate that reward to yourself.

In a moment you'll read an account of how I turned a chance encounter with pocket aces into a nearly full-blown attack of the tilts. You can judge for yourself whether it was worth the time it took to write this report, but I put it to you that recalling and recounting the experience—yes, writing it down in all its painful, shameful glory—has kept me from falling into the same trap on several occasions since. How big a reward is that? The kind that we measure in money.

Hey, everybody falls into traps from time to time, even ones of their own making, but if you're too lazy to learn from the experience, even at the cost of hard work or home-work, then you have no one to blame but yourself. *Don't* be lazy! *Do* be honest! Write down what you go through, so you don't have to go through it over and over and over again. George Satayana said, "Those who cannot remember the past are condemned to repeat it." You can remember the past. All you have to do is decide to want to.

CORKING

A friend of mine has a pet way of describing his play when his play goes south. "I am a cork," he will declare, "bobbing on the sea of poker." *Corking,* then, is his personal slang word for tilt. Of course, he would like to avoid tilt at all times, but, of course, that's easier said than done, even when we've got a clever word like *corking* to help the cause of keeping us on the straight-and-narrow path.

Here's how I went corking last night, and please note how my own good fortune triggered the near-catastrophe in the first place. After hours of muddling along with no cards, I finally picked up pocket aces in early position. Part of me said, "Slow play!" Since I had waited so long for big tickets, I wanted to make sure I got the maximum value out of them. I knew better, though, and my primary program-ming kicked in: *When you get the goods, bet the goods.* So I did. Everyone folded, leaving me with nothing to show for my aces but the puny, paltry blinds.

I kicked myself for not slow playing. Despite my under-standing of the underlying logic of the circumstance (you don't want to give a swarm of inferior hands a shot at snap-ping off your big pair), I couldn't help feeling that I had *wasted my aces.* Worse, I let that feeling infect my play, and in that instant I started corking; I began to go on tilt. Hav-ing notionally wasted my aces, I let myself believe that I'd been cheated out of chips that I somehow deserved. Looking at my next starting hand—Q-T offsuit—I allowed myself to entertain the notion that I would win with Q-T all those chips that I "deserved" to win with A-A. Have you ever heard such claptrap in all your life?

It won't take a vivid imagination to guess what happened next, for Q-T is no A-A, no matter how devoutly I wished it to be. I pushed too hard, then chased too far, and ended up losing a lot of bets to a hand (guess what?) far superior to mine.

Then I did the *very same thing* on the *very next hand.* With an even weaker holding this time! What the hell was I thinking?

Within two hands of getting the best holding in hold'em, I was a cork, bobbing on the sea of poker. Within two hands of getting a hand I thought would win me big money, I was losing big money. I was on tilt—*speed-tilt*—and heading for a major disaster. I had to take steps.

So I did, right out of the card room, and once around the casino, all the way around the property. *Big* walk. One that gave me plenty of time to think about what I'd just gone through.

My first play had been correct: I raised with aces, hoping to thin the field. In fact, I got a good outcome with that hand—they all gave up without a fight—but I treated it as a failure, and I filled myself with wistful longing and regret. Then I committed a cardinal sin of poker. I let *what happened last* affect *what happens next.* I pushed two hands too far, and gave away all my hard-fought equity in the game. Then I recovered and did something right again: I got up and walked it off. Instead of staying and playing catch-up to my catch-up, I put myself out of harm's way until I could stop corking and return to my normal, disciplined game.

Can you do this? Can you detect the onset of tilt in your

play and choke it off before it slaughters you? Can you tell when you're starting to cork, then get out of the turbulent sea while there's still time? I hope you can, because cork floats well, but nothing floats forever.

> *There are times when you want to slow-play big hands, but don't let greed cloud your judgment. Raising with big pairs to narrow the field in hold'em is like standing on 17 in blackjack; it's just sound basic strategy. Anything else would be monkey poker, and who wants to fall victim to that?*

Losing Control

Here are some ways to know when you're losing control of your game:

- A hand you folded an hour ago looks like a hand worth raising with now.
- You call a raise and a reraise before the flop with 5-6, knowing that you're up against big tickets, but banking on stealth because who'd figure you for calling with such crud?
- You call the flop and turn with bottom pair, expecting to hit trips because you're "due."
- You run hopeless bluffs, trying to get well quick.
- You know—just know—that the next rack of chips will be the one that turns things around.

Okay, those are some warning signs of tilt, but they're not the only ones. More important, they're not yours. What puts you on tilt? What turns you into a cork, bobbing on the sea of poker? Is it alcohol? Playing against maniacs? Weariness? Bad beats? You won't know unless you write it down.

When you're done writing, look at what you've written, and summarize it with a catch phrase or a watchword you can use to warn yourself when it starts to happen again. A simple, whispered, "I think I'm starting to cork here" can keep you out of mounds of money-wasting trouble.

So give yourself a word, or give yourself a phrase, but in all events give yourself a clue. It's the only way to give yourself a chance.

DEMASIADO

Demasiado is a beautiful word. *Demasiado* means "too much" in Spanish. I use this word to warn myself against the things I do too much of in poker, and you can too.

For instance, if you're like many people playing cardroom hold'em these days, you do this too much: You defend your big blind. I don't know why. Maybe you've taken some dubious math into your head that says you're always getting correct odds to call a raise in the big blind. Or perhaps it's just sheer cussed-mindedness on your part. Most likely you've become so accustomed to having your blinds attacked that you no longer give a second thought to throwing in that second bet. *Demasiado!* You do that too much! I don't care how good your so-called pot odds are, if you waste an extra bet on a codpiece like 8-3 offsuit, you're only asking to lose that extra bet. *Basta!* (That's an Italian word. It means *enough!—stop doing this right now before you hurt yourself even more, you blessed fool!*) Some blinds are worth defending. Others are not. Stop feeling like you have to defend them all, and your performance will improve.

Here's another thing I've seen you do too much: You call with weak aces. There's no denying the strength of aces, of course, but yet when you get one of those beauties in your hand, you can't seem to throw it away, no matter how weak your kicker is. It's like aces come with special glue that makes them stick to your fingers. If only your chips behaved the same way.

You know what happens to bad aces, don't you? That's right, *they lose to good aces!* When there's an ace on the flop, if no one else has an ace, you likely won't get much action, but if there *is* another ace out there, it probably has a better kicker than yours, which means you'll either win a small pot or lose a big one. So the next time you see a weak ace in your hand, just tell yourself *demasiado,* and let that loser slip.

Demasiado! You call with drawing hands against single opponents *way* too much. You'll flop a flush draw or an open-ended straight draw, and your single foe will bet. The thought will briefly cross your mind that you don't have odds to call, but you'll call anyway, because you only need *one more card* to complete your hand, and *this could be the time.* Goodness! *Demasiado!* Look, if you're even 2-1 against completing your hand, and you're only getting 1-1 return on your investment, you'll *never* make money that way. Maybe the dead money in the pot justifies your call— maybe not. Do you know for sure? If you call every time you're in this situation, I guarantee you're calling too often.

- *Demasiado:* Driving hopeless bluffs into calling stations on the river.
- *Demasiado:* Putting too much faith (and too many bets) into naked A-2s in Omaha/8.
- *Demasiado:* Playing pairs with bad kickers in seven stud or playing pairs when neither your pair nor your kicker is sufficiently live.
- *Demasiado:* Playing recklessly during the rebuy period of a tournament, following the dubious logic that one or two (or six!) more rebuys won't kill you.

- *Demasiado:* Calling with rough lows against lowball opponents known to bet smooth ones only.
- *Demasiado:* Letting yourself become distracted, annoyed, aggravated, or angry by the behavior of other players.
- *Demasiado:* Playing hunch hands.
- *Demasiado:* Taking the worst of it when you *know* you have the worst of it.

Am I wrong? Fine, I'm wrong. You don't have any of these *demasiados* in your game—but you have others. You know you do, and I'll bet you know them by heart.

Too many loose calls? Too many naked raises? Too many beers? Generate a list. When you've generated that list, take it and tape it to the dashboard of your car so that you can scan it and muse upon it en route to the place you play. Cement in your mind all of your crazy-making *demasiados* so that when you find yourself in a situation that tempts you to do the wrong thing, you can muster the awareness, courage, and strength of will to do less of the wrong thing and more of the right thing instead.

Demasiado proves the principle that less is more: Less surrender to obvious errors equals more chips for you. What could be simpler than that?

> *There must be something you do too much of. Maybe you get over-involved with small straights in stud. To break yourself of that demasiado, simply tell yourself that small straights don't exist for you today. You might lose a little equity—today—but you'll gain a lot of discipline, and that will serve you better in the end.*

Temptation

Here's some useful advice: Curb your atavistic urges.

Mr. Dictionary defines atavistic thus:

At·a·vis·tic, *adj.* of, pertaining to, or characterized by ata-vism; reverting to or suggesting the characteristics of a re mote ancestor or primitive type.

When you yield to your atavistic urges, you play primi-tive poker, the kind of sloppy, ugly, brainless poker you played when you first started out, back when you still played with wild cards maybe; back before you even knew what drawing to a bottom pair meant. Do you remember your primitive poker self? You didn't know about kicker trouble, pot odds, trap betting, or all the subtleties of the game that you now know. All you knew was that poker was *fun,* fun on some gut level, where decisions didn't matter and outcomes rested in the hands of fate.

When you play atavistic poker, you revert to old bad habits. No wonder I say curb, curb.

It's hard to curb urges because uncurbed urges feel so good. As Oscar Wilde put it, "The only way to get rid of a temptation is to yield to it." And yield we do. We yield to all sorts of unproductive and unprofitable poker moves, just because *it feels good.*

It's the truth. For instance, we just *love* flopping a big hand with bad cards, because we enjoy the look on the ko-sher players' faces when we turn over that improbable win-ner. Is this good poker? *Of course not.* Can we stop ourselves from feeling the urge? No way. Can we cease yielding to it? Maybe.

Suppose you have the habit of raising on the river with-out stopping to contemplate the ol' "only hand that can call you is one that can beat you" paradigm. You want to curb that habit, but the next time the situation comes up, you make the raise without thinking. The time after that, you do the same thing, but *that* time you remember, shortly after the fact, that this is a habit you're trying to break. Well, the situation repeats, and the next time your recognition of it comes in the middle of the act of betting. *Next* time, though, you catch yourself *before* you bet, and now the beast is tamed.

All of which requires, of course, dedication to curbing temptation and not yielding to it. That could be tough. "I can resist everything," said Oscar Wilde, "except temptation."

SCABS

Suppose you had a scab on your knee. Your impulse would be to pick it—and you know how good it would feel if you did. Very common behavior, indulging ourselves in something that feels good. It doesn't have to be a scab. It could be coffee, cigarettes, booze, pot, porn, anything. Whatever floats your boat. Why? Because self-indulgence, as they say, is its own reward. Now, I have no problem with self-indulgence—*after* you play poker. That's when it's time to enjoy the fruits of your labor with a beer or a chocolate bar or whatever, but when self-indulgence happens while you're still in the game, that's a recipe for mayhem.

Self-Indulgence Scenario "A"

You go heads-up against some evildoing blind-stealing "sumbitch," calling his raise even though you have only a scabby 7-4 with which to defend. The flop comes J-8-4 and you get all moist and oozy because now you have bottom pair—good enough to beat the pure bluff that you mistakenly put your opponent on. Why? Because you're feeling pushed around and can't fight the urge to push back. You want to make the bastard pay for bullying your blind. Most of the time, though, the bastard doesn't pay. His hand is legitimate, and our desire to feel good is thwarted by the sad facts of probability. Then we end up losing not just money, but also credibility, image, *self*-image, and control. So now we have a new math:

> *Self-indulgence = self-destruction.*

Self-Indulgence Scenario "B"

You're getting ready to leave a game, but you decide to just play through to your blind before you go. This feels good because it feels as if you're getting something for nothing, a free ride, a look at several more hands without having to pay the price of the blinds. Trouble is, you've already mentally checked out of the game, and your chances of playing Killer Poker (or even adequate poker) have checked out too. So now here comes a hand—say 7-5—the number of your high school football jersey. You know you shouldn't play it, and never ever would play it except for the fact that you're already halfway outta there. Maybe you have a few extra chips above some arbitrary number of chips (three more than a full rack, say) so you decide to take a flier on the hand.

Why? It's because it feels good. It's *action!* That last hit of action before you have to hit the road. Then—sad story— you catch a piece of the flop, make several calls you shouldn't make, and end up getting clobbered, which you probably deserved, since you probably had no business calling in the first place. Now smarting from that wound, you decide to take another lap or two (or six) around the table, rather than leave the game you had previously decided to leave. An hour or two (or six) later, you stumble away, stunned and remorseful, having turned a nice respectable win into a devastating loss. You started out doing something that you thought would make you feel good and ended up feeling bad, bad, bad.

Never fall victim to this again! Vow now to play all hands and every hand for strategy, not self-indulgence. Set this as your goal: Be in there for a reason, not just because you feel like picking a scab.

Unless, of course, it's the other guy's scab.

Because as we've already discussed, since everything you feel is pretty much the same stuff that everyone else feels, you can reliably predict that a certain number of your foes are doing things at the poker table *just to feel good about themselves, too.* You can use this against them. You can manipulate them into making countless costly mistakes in service of that spurious need.

A guy hates to have his blind attacked? All the more reason to attack it! His defense makes him feel proud and bold and strong, even though it's frequently a big, fat, hairy error to defend.

Someone to your left looks as if she's about to leave the game and is just playing through to her blinds? Don't raise in front of her. Encourage her to call, since she wants to blow off a few random chips before she goes and will likely choose to blow them off with a marginal hand. Don't encourage her to wise up or tighten up. Let her toss her loose, dead money in the pot. *Then bet any flop.* She won't call, not if it means breaking her rack, and if she does break her rack, maybe you can get her stuck for the whole hundred chips!

Remember: Every mistake you discover in your own play is one that's present in many enemies' plays as well. Track their self-indulgences. I'll start your list for you.

- They berate their foes or their dealers.
- They give lessons at the table.
- They call raised pots with bad hands.

- They take slim draws.
- They show their "smart laydowns" to the dealer or other players.
- They raise blind after a bad beat.
- They play drunk or stoned.
- They throw or bend or break the cards.

What I want you to do, and I'm not kidding about this, is to photocopy this image:

Next, cut out the words and glue them to a poker chip. Keep this chip where you can see it while you play. Do you think this is a ridiculous waste of paper, paste, time, and chip? Hey, if this simple exercise keeps me from picking even one scab per session, or helps me exploit even one other player's weakness in this area, then I kind of figure it's worth it. Maybe that's just me, but then again I'm prepared to do anything, even waste time or look ridiculous, if I think it'll help my poker. How about you? Are you interested in winning play? Or would you rather just feel good?

Here's a challenge: Find a limit you now consider "beneath you" and go play your best game there. The hard part of this is that playing your best doesn't feel that good when you're playing for insignificant stakes. The point of the exercise is to discover that performance, not *stakes, is what matters.*

Rage Assuagers

Does it seem strange to equate anger with self-indulgence, especially when self-indulgence is something we do to make ourselves feel good? When a player throws cards at the dealer, he would seem to be about as far from feeling good as he could get. So how is this act self-indulgent? Here's how: When he throws those cards, he's not so much demonstrating anger as he is trying to assuage his rage. He is, in short, using an act of fury to make himself feel better.

How forked up is that? Very extremely. Let's look inside this hothead's head and see what he's thinking.

> Well, the fricking dealer did it to me again. Dealt me a sweet pair of kings, only to ruin everything by flopping an ace. That dealer hates me. In fact, the cards hate me. In fact, the whole universe hates me, and the only measure of revenge I can get right now is to throw these cards at that dealer and hope to hit the universe on the rebound. There! Now I feel better!

We know that it's bad form to throw cards at dealers. It's bad for the dealer, bad for the game, bad for the club, bad for poker, and bad for the universe in general. We now know something else: When a player acts badly he's trying to *feel better*. Use this information against him! Reinforce in him the idea that the most important thing for him to do right now is to *try to feel better*. Obviously the more energy he invests in his feelings, the less energy he can invest in recovering his equilibrium and returning to perfect play. Help him invest his energy in his feelings! Commiserate over his bad beat. Be sympathetic to his plight. Agree with him that his universe is a hostile, arbitrary, and ultimately unfair place. The more he thinks like this, the more you can prove him right with superior play. He might actually weep on the way home. I guess that's not your problem, is it?

3

♣ ♠ ♦ ♥

CARDS IN CONTEXT

♣ ♠ ♦ ♥

POISON

Little cards are poison in hold'em. You know this to be true, but maybe you don't know *how* true.

First, let's state a prime directive of Killer Poker:

> *Loose call bad.*
> *Loose raise good.*

Take this directive to mean that in most cases you'd rather be raising than just calling pre-flop. This puts a burden on you since, having raised pre-flop, you'll be expected to continue to drive the action post-flop. If you fail to do this, your opponents will quickly figure out how to beat you. They'll simply call any raise and bet any check. The strength you represent with a pre-flop raise is thwarted by the weakness you subsequently show, and the whole point of being known as an aggressive player will be neutralized by your lack of follow-through.

So you want to be able to follow through with a post-flop bet more often than not. Here's where your big cards come in. If you raise pre-flop with big cards, several good things can happen. You might, of course, hit the flop. Big cards plus more big cards equal big hand. Even if the flop comes with medium cards or littles, you may still be able to bet, since you still have the chance of hitting an overcard to complete your hand (if it's not already good as-is).

Consider Q-J, suited or unsuited. The run-of-the-monkey players will call automatically with this hand if there's a large field and an unraised pot. What they fail to understand is that this is the sort of hand with which you can easily *take control*, assuming that you raise pre-flop, for then its strength is not in straight or flush draws but in sheer high-card muscle, wedded to a raise.

Suppose you do. Suppose you raise pre-flop with Q-J. If you get a bunch of calls from a bunch of sheep, you know that you're up against anything from weak aces and kings all the way down to ground chuck like 8-7 and baby pairs. Now here comes the flop. With big cards you can (in certain circumstances) comfortably raise any high, middle, or low flop.

If you start out with littles, the situation is exactly reversed. Suppose you've taken this whole Killer Poker thing *way too far* and find yourself raising pre-flop with something like 6-5 suited. If high cards come, you can't bet the flop for fear of betting into big pairs. If a middle flop comes, you can't feel too comfy betting because your best holding is likely to be a straight draw or weak flush draw. On the other hand, your foes could be in there with the straight or flush draw, *plus* a working pair, *or* overpairs, *or* big tickets looking to hit an overcard on the turn or the river.

So naturally you desire a low flop, coordinated to your little cards. However, even if you get the flop you want, you still have an uphill climb.

> *The real problem with little cards is this: Even if you get the flop you want, you're nowhere near home-free.*

Suppose you're holding that ugly 6-5 and hit a six on the flop. Your top pair isn't likely to be *the* top pair, and if it is, you're vulnerable to overcards or straight draws or made straights. If you check in that instance, you're exposing weakness and leaving yourself vulnerable to attack. That's no good. If you bet, you risk hearing about it from someone with a bigger hand. Sadness!

Of course, you *could* flop a set with your raggedy littles. In which case all you have to worry about are set-over-sets, straights, flushes, and full houses. How comfortable do you feel now? About the only time you feel truly at ease with a low flop is when it absolutely makes your hand—you flop a straight, say—but how much action are you likely to get on a flop which hits you so hard that it misses everyone else?

Littles are poison. *Poison!* With big cards, you can hit your flop and be good enough to win right there. With littles, you can hit your flop and still have to hope it holds up till the river. To put it most succinctly, little cards offer too much headroom for the rest of the deck.

So why do you play littles in the first place? Maybe, frankly, from listening to me too much. Here I am, the proponent of Killer Poker, saying that any cards are playable under the right circumstances. This is true—*under the right circumstances*. If I have reason to believe that I can fold the field and get heads up against a blind or two (whom I have reason to believe I can outplay after the flop), why then I'll raise with anything. Big cards, little cards, bingo cards—I don't care. Because in that instance, I'm not raising on the strength of my hand, I'm raising on the combined strength of my raise and weakness of my foes. I intend to bet any flop (within reason) to try to get the random-handed blinds to run scared. This ploy may or may not work, but you can see that it's not card-dependent.

We get into trouble with littles when we depend on

them too much. We think we're being clever Killer Poker people when we raise in late position with crabgrass. After three players have called the raise, we're suddenly praying for a miracle flop to come to rescue our sorry, overplaying asses. But the flop isn't a miracle. It comes just good enough (or just bad enough) to keep us involved in the pot. We bet the flop because it's expected of us. Then the turn kicks out one of the *many* cards that can scare us, and now the horizon turns dark. Maybe we try to keep driving, but a check-raise on the turn slows us down or drives us off and we lose once again to a hand that, unlike ours, had some actual business being in there in the first place.

Poker is a delicate dance of knowing when to stick your neck out and when to turn turtle. What started out as a pure bluff can turn into a disastrous defense of a little pair if you don't know what you're doing. So please, please, please *know what you're doing!* Study your opponents. Know who will fold under pressure. Know who only calls with premium cards. Know who calls any river. Know who likes to check-raise, and who likes to check-raise bluff. If you know your foes, and fit your play into the game accordingly, you can do almost anything. But if you don't take the time and make the effort to get a line on your opponents, then your moves will fail because they're directed at exactly the wrong player at precisely the wrong time.

Above all, *know yourself!* Know if you're prone to trying to do too much with too little. Treat your little cards like the poison they are, and this vexing little problem will probably vex you less—at least a *little* less.

> *Look inward, but also outward. Sure, ask, "Do I*
> *have a raise-worthy hand?" but also ask,*
> *"Do I have raise-worthy foes?" You can often*

succeed when you have only the hand or only the foe, but you rarely succeed when you don't have either one.

A Little Tell

There's a tell you can get off some players, one worth watching for, that relates to the play of little poison. Sometimes you'll see an opponent look at his first card and then muck his hand (or mentally muck, a decision betrayed by his body language) without even looking at the second card. In this circumstance, you can be sure that here is a player who understands the danger of little poison. He knows that if his first card is small, then he's not going to play the hand even if the second card is a suited ace or a pair card. Well! This is valuable information, no doubt. It tells you, beyond fear of contradiction, that if this player is in a hand, he's in there with the top half of the deck. That's a hell of an edge for you.

Why does a player do this? Why would any sane combatant look at just one card and then wave a big flag to his foes saying, "See? I couldn't care less about this!" The answer lies in our earlier observation about some players' need to feel good about themselves. When a player thus burdened with need looks at his first card and dismisses the hand on that basis, he's telling himself, "See how disciplined I am?" He's showing off to himself, trying to impress himself with his own stern restraint.

Well, good for him. Meanwhile, he has just opened up a great gaping hole through which you can suck his money. Now you know that any hand he holds contains two big cards. When the flop comes big, you can get away. When the flop comes little, you can attack. He can't defend unless and until the board improves, and when it does improve, you'll know where he's at. This player isn't capable of flopping a small set, because he *never* plays small pairs. That's a huge edge for you.

Obviously you don't want to give your enemies that kind of edge in return. If your calling requirements are stringent, it's easy for you to know that you've given up on a hand. It's also very easy—too damn easy—to betray this information to attentive foes. So even if you hate your little cards, it's crucial that you remain poised, patient, and cool. Examine and consider each hand as if it were pocket aces, and fold each hand you choose to fold with the same neutral grace. You don't need to show off to yourself or impress yourself with the correctness of your play. Leave that to the lesser minds.

Don't ignore the small-card leak in your game. It's a throwback to that old hold'em idea that "any two cards can win." You don't still believe that, do you? If you do, let's stay with the subject a little while longer.

ABSOLUT

When you start treating little cards like the poison they are in hold'em, an interesting phenomenon takes place. With a righteous awareness of little poison, you start to view with contempt every single 2, 3, 4, 5, 6, 7, or even 8 you hold. You begin to consider more than half the deck (28/52 to be exact, or 54 percent) to be unworthy of your admiration or even consideration. You start to hate those cards.

Good! You've eliminated the bad half of the deck. Suddenly, inevitably, the quality of your starting hands—let's call it the *purity* of your starting hands—goes way up. The Swedish language has a word for this purity: *absolut*. It doesn't mean exactly the same as our *absolute* (and, of course, has nothing but brand-naming to do with vodka). The Swedish word *absolut* implies a degree of maximum, total, unblemished perfection. So then let's imagine that there's such a thing as an *absolut* deck, one containing only A, K, Q, J, T, and 9. This (for the sake of this exercise) is the deck you play, while meanwhile your foes are still playing that regular deck, the one contaminated by all that little poison. Can you see how this difference will manifest itself over time? They're playing crap, or at least half-crap; you aren't.

Perhaps you think playing the *absolut* deck will make you too tight a player. That's fine—you can stand to play tighter. I'm not talking about cutting back on your raises; to the contrary, I'm talking about a way to ensure that your raises *always* have at least a little muscle behind them—and a way to ensure that your calls stop being ridiculous.

So how does playing an *absolut* deck actually change your play? What sort of hands will you no longer fart around with?

Any two unpaired littles, for starters, and this includes suited cards, connected cards, and those hopeless suited connectors that bring you so much grief. Will you miss the stupid connectors? Not at all. Remember: In the real world you're just as likely to pick up suited K-Q as suited 6-5. If you're playing an *absolut* deck, you're just a lot less likely (like 100 percent less likely) to get pounded by the bad hand, while you still get to profit from the good. (**Caveat:** There are no nevers in Killer Poker. If you're on the button and it's a family pot, you can see the flop with 6-5 suited; if you're stealing a blind, you can raise with 6-5 or any brick-brick, but those are exceptions, not the rule.)

Now then, if littles are poison, they are also contagious poison. They contaminate any high card they come in contact with. K-3? The three makes the king as toxic as an EPA

Superfund site. Treat the hand like the poison it is, and you will save *so much* money. And please don't cry "suited!" Suited gives you an extra few percent of value—and an extra few percent of nothing is nothing. Starting with suited cards, you're 8-1 against flopping a four-flush. So if you go to battle with something like T-6, the fact that it's suited is irrelevant to subsequent play *almost all the time.* Even when that flush gets there, you can't push it too aggressively for fear of running into a bigger flush. Such is the misery of little poison.

Needless to say, playing the *absolut* deck will minimize your legitimate beats. Why would you want to play Q-4 anyhow? So you can flop two pair and get snapped off by a real two pair?

So what about little pairs? How playable are they? Is a poison seven neutralized by another seven? Maybe—if you can limp in for a single bet and flop a set, then maybe. Again, you're almost 8-1 against flopping a set with your starting pair, so most of the time you won't improve. Set-over-set is much more likely when you start with a small pair than with a big one. How much trouble are you looking for? I'm assuming that *discipline* is an ongoing challenge for you. Let yourself screw around with little pairs and soon you'll go back to screwing around with 5-4 suited. Once you make that hand playable, can 5-2 suited be far behind? Be strong. Just say no to littles—even to little pairs.

Which leaves only the combination of ace-little for our contemplation. Is an ace an antidote to little poison? Is a suited ace? Again, the answer is maybe. If you find yourself among a herd of promiscuous callers and infrequent raisers in the sort of game where any flopped ace will hold up, then maybe. Quality players, however, will kill you with kickers. Why invite the torment? Muck your ace-little, too.

I know you're in love with A-4 suited. Some time back in the last century you held A-4 suited and flopped a straight flush, and you've loved that hand ever since. That was then. This is now. Be honest with yourself. If discipline is a problem, it's up to you to find a solution. Consider the *absolut* deck to be your remedial retraining.

You know, overweight people frequently go hunting for the perfect diet. They try low fat and then low carbs. They limit sugars. Then they limit starch. They eat strange, over-priced "nutrition" bars and drink strange milkshakes that taste like nothing so much as blended chalk. Nothing seems to work. Why? Because they already *know* what not to eat—they just can't follow through. Killer Poker is about knowing, but it's also about doing.

So think of this as your *absolut* hold'em diet. It's one you may find you can stick to. Like any diet, of course, there are times you can go off it and not pay too high a price. Often, the point of the diet is not to lose weight, but rather to demonstrate to yourself your strength of will and self-control. It's the same with the *absolut* deck.

So next time you play hold'em, imagine that your ab-horrence of little cards is almost religious in its fervor. See how long you can go without putting any voluntary money into any pot with any hand containing any 8, 7, 6, 5, 4, 3, or 2. The longer you go before giving in, the higher you score in this exercise.

You'll remember that we ran a similar exercise earlier, when I asked you to play a game called "Raise!" where the goal was to raise as much as possible, and your liberal rais-ing made you a winner in the hidden game that only you knew you were playing. Treat *absolut* the same way. See how thoroughly you can detach from little poison, and re-ward yourself accordingly.

> *Can you play an* absolut *deck for an entire*
> *session? Forget about winning and losing, do it*
> *to demonstrate discipline. The improvement to*
> *your self-image—*I'm an iron-willed player—*will*
> *be valuable to your poker no matter what*
> *the monetary outcome.*

When to Play Littles

Obviously there are times when it's correct to play little cards. If you're last to act in a multiple-way pot, you'll be delighted to throw in a single bet with small suited connectors or some little pair. You know that all sorts of good flops can happen for you, and you also know that you're cagey enough to get away from the myriad bad flops that can happen. In other words, you have a clear enough understanding of correct play to know when you can afford to play incorrectly. Yes, you have this understanding—but maybe your understanding needs periodic refreshment. That's when it's useful to have a reliable, set-and-forget mode of play to fall back on. For the times when we forget the difference between good hands and bad hands, a system like *absolut* can keep us from getting reamed by our own transient cluelessness.

Assuming—*assuming*—you know the rules, you can sometimes afford to break them. For the times you forget, let little poison be your guide. Playing hands that contain only 9s and above will guarantee that you never get too far out of line. Just tell yourself, "If it's low, it's got to go." Your discipline (and your bankroll) will thank you.

RUNS

Every poker player gets the runs from time to time. Not that kind of runs (although there's no telling what kind of gastrointestinal havoc all those comped casino meals can cause). No, the runs I'm talking about are runs of cards, runs of luck, and other runs like these . . .

Running Good

If only this run ran your way more often, right? When you're running good, your bluffs work out and your hands hold up. It's not just luck, of course, that makes someone run good. Rather it's that heady combination of luck, skill, experience, and expertise. Sure it's great when the cards break your way, but if the only time you run good is when you're running lucky, then you're bound to run down at last.

> *If you're running good,* keep *running. Either they're playing badly or you're playing well; in any case, this is the time to stay in action. Don't let the fear of giving back some gains keep you from maximizing your profit.*

Running Scared

Running scared is where you arrive when you've been running bad. Certain that the card gods curse you, you default to a timid, reactive playing style. You become convinced that Murphy's Law was passed just to punish you for the arrogance of believing you actually knew how to play this game. The trouble with running scared is that it actually reinforces running bad. If you're running scared, there's one thing you must do to solve the problem: Don't play. Just don't. Not until you can approach the poker table with the élan required to ensure that the other players routinely run scared from you.

> *Winning poker requires courage and you can't have courage if you're running scared. In this circumstance, gear down to a smaller limit or find something else to do with your time.*

Bombing Runs

You've seen this happen: A player catches a few cards and suddenly he's on fire. On every hand, he's in there with a bet and a raise. If you try to slow him down by playing back at him, he just plays back at you, leaving you feeling vulnerable and attacked; in short, shell-shocked. He's on a bombing run, and as long as the run lasts, he has a tremendous advantage over you. What's the edge? He's on top, hurling bets and raises down at you. All things considered, you're much better off being the bomber than the bombee, and if you can't get out of the way of the bombs, get out of the game. In that circumstance, why would you *not* leave? Is it ego? Is it attitude? Or is it the firm (if misguided) belief that the bomber will suddenly cease firing? Sometimes I think it's sheer laziness, inertia, or chair glue. Do not stay in a bad game! Get up and move. Leave the club if you have to. Only a fool lets himself get bombed into oblivion when he doesn't have to.

> *If you find yourself on a bombing run,* keep bombing. *The key to a really big win is that one pot you capture in the middle of your rush just because you were* on *a rush and thus took control of the game.*

The Runaround

Sometimes you just don't know where an opponent is at. When you think he's bluffing he's got a monster. When you're convinced he's for real he taunts you by turning over his rags after you fold. Time after time he's got you leaning the wrong way, because he's always one step ahead of you in his thinking. Is he smarter than you? Maybe. If he is, then it's no trick for him to outthink you, and thus give you the runaround. In due course, he will take your money—all of it. What's the solution? Go find someone dumber than you and outthink them instead. Don't let your pride keep you in a contest you can't win. Like bombing runs, it's much better to be giving the runaround than getting it.

> *When you have your foe leaning the wrong way, keep pushing. Poker is a game of decisions, and if your opponent is in a position where he lacks clarity or confidence in his choices, you want him to have to make as many (potentially wrong) choices as possible.*

Run of the Mill

How good a player are you, really? Do you constantly get to the middle rounds of a tournament, only to stall out before you reach the final table? Could it be that you're really, at the end of the day, only run of the mill? In poker, and especially in poker tournaments, average achievement just doesn't get the job done. What can you do to not be run of the mill? Work on your game. Study poker books and run poker simulations. Think about your game and talk about your game. Write about your game. Improve your game by doing the exercises in this book. In sum: Drag yourself kicking and screaming from a comfortable mediocrity to a higher level of achievement.

Change-management consultants speak of *the pain of the*

present. Unless the pain of the present is sufficiently great, there's no real motivation for anyone to change. Sadly, run-of-the-mill players may not be *bad enough* to stimulate a revolution in their play. In poker, as in life, just good enough, just *isn't* good enough. Run hard, or don't run at all.

> *There's tremendous overlooked value in rereading the books in your poker library. Books that you read as a beginner will offer you powerful new insights now that you know the game from a different and much more experienced point of view.*

Run Off at the Mouth

Some players talk better than they play, but some players play better because of *how* they talk. You have, I'm sure, sat next to one of these white noise generators. No matter what words come out of his mouth, the net effect is to put you off your game. Why? Because you're devoting at least some of your attention to what the yammerhead has to say, and that's at least some of your attention that you're not devoting to your game. Some players use talk as a tactic. They know that the more they talk the more you listen, the more you listen the less you concentrate, and the less you concentrate the more prone you are to making mistakes. Wear headphones or change seats if you have to, but don't let the chatterers get inside your head. That's exactly where they want to be.

> *Try wearing headphones—and then listen to nothing at all. The chatterboxes will shut up because you "plainly" can't hear them, but at the*

same time you won't miss any potentially valuable audio tells. People may, in fact, become careless about their talk (like telling the dealer what they really had, or emitting audible sighs) because they think you can't hear them.

Running Riot—or—Running a Fever

In certain places, at certain times, a certain madness can overwhelm a game. Suddenly everyone is calling every raise. When this happens, hand values go down and fluctuations go up, up, up. It is, of course, possible to beat up on a game that's running riot, but it requires some adjustment and some real discipline on your part.

First, even though everyone else seems to be serially raising with garbage, you must not fall prey to the same fever. Keep your own starting requirements high. You don't have to worry about the other players not giving action to a tighty like you; they're so far into the fever that they don't even know what tight looks like.

Second, recognize that with so many people calling so many raises, a lot of garbage hands are going to be getting correct odds to call. You'll need to hit your hand, and hit it hard, in order to win the big pots that a fever game offers. Frustration is high—but profit is too—when a game runs riot.

When a game is extremely raisey, you'll need both more chips and more perseverance. If your mindset or your wallet can't stand the fluctuations of a fever game, go find a tamer game and play in that one instead. Otherwise, buy that extra rack of chips and strap in for the ride.

The Long Run

Did you win last night? That's terrific. Who cares? Don't tell me (or yourself, or your mother, or lover, or anyone else, except possibly your dog) how much money you won last night. Last night doesn't matter. How did you do last week, last month, last year, last decade? Either you're a winning player or you're not, and the jury won't return a verdict on that question for a long, long time. Bring your best game to the table every time you come to the table. Work to improve the game you bring. Stay after your goals for years and years, and *then* talk about results. Running good doesn't matter. Running bad doesn't matter. Running lucky couldn't possibly matter less. Running over your opponents is important, but running true and running smooth are worth even more. Don't run yourself ragged and don't run yourself down, and you're bound to run hot overall.

> *Running good or running bad is more a matter of the card player than the cards. To prove this to yourself, simply record every hand you hold for several sessions. Even in this unscientific sample, you'll see that your distribution of premium hands and rags is pretty much the same pretty much every time out.*

Run It Past Again

Remember, you just have to win—you don't have to win right now. Your every adjustment to circumstances should be geared toward the long-term goal of being a winning player. This means that you ignore bad beats and lucky suck-outs alike, except as a function of how the information surrounding those outcomes can improve your play and the exploitation of your foes.

At the same time, don't confuse good luck with good play. A key card at the right time can put you several hundred chips ahead for a session. When that happens—when the racks are piled unusually high in front of you—it's easy to believe that you have once and for all entered the blessed realm of superior skill. Don't be fooled! A careful analysis of these big-win sessions will identify the source of your prosperity as a combination of correct plays and fortunate outcomes. No one wins on skill alone, and it's a toxic sort of self-delusion to believe that, in all instances, skill can overcome bad card-falls.

What skill does is minimize damage. What skill does is maximize opportunity. What skill does is smooth out the bumps that luck lays down in the road. What skill mostly does is give you the confidence to make the right play at the right time. Skill, in other words, reinforces strength and cancels fear.

When your game is informed by skill, skill derived from hard study and long experience, you feel secure in the choices you make. You feel certain that your choices are sensible ones, backed up by your understanding of yourself, your foes, and the underlying math of the game. With skill on your side, your choices are not tainted by insecurity or doubt. Skill, then, keeps you on your balance, plus it gives you the power to put other players off theirs, and that is a beautiful thing indeed.

WOBBLE

The worst thing you can do in poker is to be weak. It kills you two ways, by yielding initiative and by leaving you open to attack.

In certain games in certain circumstances, all you have to do is *bet* to *win*. Strong players understand this intuitively. The rest of us watch and wonder how those stron-gies got so rich. The answer is simple: They seize the initiative, where less strong and less secure players do not.

I hear you complaining and I know your beef. You claim that every time you try to seize such initiative, you get run down by some J-5 moleskin who doesn't know enough to throw away that cheese against your monster raise. Sorry about that. Cheese happens, but wouldn't you rather be in a game where the moleskins play J-5 than in a game where they don't? So when you're there, *play strong!* This keeps the initiative where it belongs—*with you!*

Plus, I'll bet they don't draw out on you as often as you think they do. There is such a thing in this world as con-firmation bias: We're more likely to see what we expect to see, exactly *because* we expect to see it. Suck-outs imprint themselves on our minds, to the point where we start to see them everywhere we look. This gives us both an exagger-ated fear of suck-outs, as well as a reinforced rationale for continued timidity and weak play. Which is, of course, ex-actly opposite to successful strategy in poker.

Look, either you're strong or you're weak. If you're strong, you attack and punish the weak. If you're weak, alas, you're meat. Strong players test everyone by means of at-tack. They probe you just to see if you're weak. They want to know what you're made of, and they're not afraid of spending a few bets to find out. The truth is revealed under pressure, and they want to know the truth of you. They want, in short, to see if you will *wobble.*

Here's how it happens. Here's how your incipient weak-ness can get you into trouble at the hands of a strong, skilled player who wants nothing from the situation except to test your mettle. It's a hypothetical situation, but I'll bet if you're honest with yourself you'll admit that it's not as hypothetical as all that.

You've bought into a $10–$20 hold'em game for moderate money—$500—and you're playing what you perceive to be tight-aggressive poker. You throw away such holdings as K-little, 9-8 suited, bad aces. You don't mind making a few folds. You want a tight image and you also want to get the measure of your foes before you plunge into the fray.

Now here comes a hand where you see pocket nines, and you decide to play it strongly with a raise. Boom! The foe to your left raises you back almost before your chips have left your hand, and you start to sweat. Does he have an overpair? Or big tickets? What is he doing in "your" pot in the first place?

Testing you, that's what. Pressing you. Messing with your mind. He sees that you haven't been involved up till now and he wants to see what you're made of—on his terms, not yours. He's been waiting for you to enter a pot, just so he could isolate you by reraising behind you. He achieves his goal: Everyone folds back around to you and you just call, wondering *what could he possibly have?*

He could have *anything*. Anything from 7-2 to pocket aces. His purpose here is simply to put your feet to the fire—a purpose that any two cards will serve. Now the flop comes T-x-x. You check, which would be a sensible thing to do in a less aggressive game. Here, though, it's just an open invitation for him to bet, and he does because, again, he's not betting his hand at all. He's betting yours. He knows that almost any flop can look like a scary flop to you, when reinforced in your mind by the fact of his pre-flop reraise. Mostly he's betting that you haven't hit your hand—and since everyone misses more often than they hit, he's probably right about that. That's why the so-called *wobble raise* is so effective. Since you're more likely to miss any flop than hit it, you're more likely to wobble than not.

Do you see the razor's edge you stand on? If you surrender here, your foe knows that you're weak. He knows that you'll wobble. He knows that you'll fold under pressure. You've surrendered initiative. You are, in a word, toast.

Take a look at that flop. Take a *look* at that flop. Fit it into your foe's hand. Remember, he's no more likely to have a big hand than you are. So what's he betting on? He's betting on either a piece of the flop or no piece of the flop. *Those are the only possibilities.* Maybe he has overcards. Maybe he has a good ten. Maybe he has a pair of threes or even less. He doesn't care. He's bound to push you no matter what.

What if you push back?

I think you have to. I don't think you can afford a whiff of wobble in the sort of game where they attack wobble just because it's there. You're assailed on all sides. Until you throw some muscle back at your assailants, they're not going to let up. I wouldn't. Would you? Of course not. It's what you dream of: tough guy poker—not just Killer Poker but super-duper killer-diller poker.

You fantasize about playing this tough. You fantasize about being the one who makes others wobble, but then when you get into a situation where you *can* be the one, you blow it completely. How does that happen?

Suppose you drop back to a much lower level, a place where you feel comfortable splashing bets around because the money is well within your comfort zone. You play strong—*and it works!* Next thing you know, you're the bully in the game. You're the one putting others on the wobble. You're the one with all the big stacks. You are, in short, the King of Cheese! That's when you're doomed.

It's because in that instant you stop playing strong poker and start playing glory poker. You're not earning money; you're earning admiration—so you think. Haven't you figured it out yet? Each of us is the center of our own universe, and we're of abiding slender interest to the universe next door.

No one *cares* how well you do; no one *cares* how good you feel; but you don't care that they don't care. You're too busy shining, basking in your own marvelous ability. You're not playing Killer Poker or perfect poker or even semiadequate poker. You're just showing off. Before you know it, you've blown off some bets and taken some beats, and find yourself back on the wobble again.

The heat of combat is not the time to stroke the ego. The heat of combat is also not the time to feel fear. The heat of combat is the time to execute. Execute plans you've made based on strategies you've devised. Play strong because *you* are strong, not because your cards are. Can you do that? Can you play without ego, but also without fear, so that you make the best possible decision based on the best available information, all the time and every time?

Also: Can you reform your thinking so that cards matter less than situations? Can you muster the strength to be a bully when bully behavior is called for? Then you've got a shot. Then the one who wobbles won't be you.

> *For your entire next session, raise every new player's first hand no matter what cards you hold. You may or may not win with this move, but you will get to see yourself as someone who is capable of moves, capable of putting others on the wobble, and that's the sort of player you definitely want to be.*

ANTIFISH

In poker, there are two basic states we can occupy: proactive or reactive. A lot of people play reactive poker. They spend a lot of time and energy getting to know their opponents, getting a line on their play. This is time well spent and energy well spent, no doubt, but another school of thought contends that if your game is all about reacting to other people's games, then you're giving away the huge advantage of initiative. In poker, in general, you'd rather be the one pushing than the one being pushed.

Take the simple act of betting. If you bet, you can get called by a better hand or a worse hand, or you can get no calls at all and win the pot right there. If you're calling, of course, the last possibility is eliminated. You may be calling with the best hand or the worst hand but in any case you're never calling with the *only* hand. The bettor can win the pot with the best hand or by driving the best hand away. The caller can win with the best hand and the best hand only. This is why people bluff.

Beyond bluffing, this is why successful players take an aggressive stance in their game. They know that there are situations where they're going to call anyhow, so they might as well bet first, just on the off-chance that their opponents have no stomach for battle. This is called bringing the fight to your enemy. When you do this, you put your enemy on the defensive. He may be able to survive in a defensive mode, but he won't be able to *thrive*.

The best offense is often a good pretense. The appearance of strength is frequently as good as the real thing. You say you can't be an aggressive poker player; you say it's not in your nature. I say that even if you don't *feel* aggressive, you can *act* aggressive. The repeated manifestation of apparent strength will lead to the development of genuine strength over time.

So how do you manifest strength you don't have? Consider the *antifish*.

I'm sure you've heard this, *"If you look around the table*

and you can't spot the fish, it's you." Hey, we've all been the fish at one time or another, but mostly we've gotten over that. Now let's take it to the next level and not only avoid *being the fish* but actually become the *antifish,* the one who runs the game.

Nature, as we know, abhors a vacuum, and a poker game without an antifish is a particularly abhorrent vacuum just waiting to be filled. Consider this: You enter a nice, friendly mid-limit hold'em game where everyone is more or less behaving themselves. They're tight, they're quiet, they're folding bad hands, and they're raising with good ones. No one's getting too frisky or too far out of line. That's a stable game. That game could go on for hours without anyone getting too badly hurt or anyone (save the house) making any serious coin.

Now here you come, the antifish, to destabilize the game. You're on a mission, filled with fiendish delight, because you know the havoc you're about to wreak. You do it because you know that the mere act of destabilizing this game, putting other players outside their comfortable little zones of expectation, will do more to make you a winner here than all the great cards you could wait and hope to catch. You do it on your very first hand, with the very first blind you post.

Ah, the first blind: Most fish, with most hands, are hoping that they won't face a raise here because, let's face it, how premium is that very first holding likely to be? They would be happy to see a flop without having to spend any more chips. Who knows? They might get lucky, flop big, and win their very first hand. That would certainly start the session off on the right foot, wouldn't it?

Actually, it wouldn't. Hoping for an unraised blind and a hot flop is about as wrong-footed as you can start out. Why? Because it says that your game is about luck, playing tidy, and hoping to catch cards. In those circumstances you can't win unless you catch cards. That means, more often than not, *you won't win.*

Enter the antifish, the player with a whole different agenda. You don't care about the chips in your blind. You're more interested in seizing the game by the throat than in winning a particular hand or saving a handful of chips. So when the action comes around to you, you *make* that raise, you pop your own blind, no matter what cards you hold. Immediately the table holds you in suspicion: "Where did you come from, nasty antifish, and where do you get off making so rash and reckless a move as to raise your own blind when everyone else was content to let you see the flop for free? Have you no gratitude? We hate you, antifish; you're ruining our fun."

Contemplate what the other players are feeling right now. Some may be angry; some may be wary; and some may be licking their chops over you because they see you as reckless and stupid, not the bold and smart antifish you really are. They're all morsels for your meal, poor fish, because they've stopped thinking about their own game and started thinking about yours instead. This is what you want; this is control—and it comes at so little cost.

Because what's the worst that can happen when you raise your own blind? The flop could miss you completely. Then you fold, and (mis)identify yourself as someone who plays too fast before the flop and pays for it afterward. That's an image you can parlay into profit later with authentically muscular hands. If you hit a flop coordinated to the arbitrarily ragged hand you raised with, why then you can drive and drive and drive, and never look like anyone but someone trying to make a hopeless bluff stand up. When you turn over misfit winners, you make the rest of the table deride, loathe, and fear you, all at the same time.

As they struggle to recover, they realize only dimly what you already know to be true: The antifish is here, and the antifish rules!

If you intend to play this role, make sure you know what you're doing, for there's a fine line between fish and anti-fish, and it is ignorance that blurs that line. So how can you tell if you're the fish or the antifish? That's easy. The fish calls a lot, folds a little, and doesn't raise at all. The antifish raises a lot, folds a lot, and almost never just calls.

Bump it or dump it *is the mantra of the antifish.*

To be the antifish, the dominant player at the table, you must be the one who is expected to raise. To create that expectation, simply put the heat on and keep it on. If you're in the right game with the right actions, you'll be the Lone Raiser—a consummation devoutly to be wished for.

I mean, really, wouldn't you like it to be that way? Wouldn't you love to play in a game where you are, literally, the only one who thinks to raise? Can't you just count the advantages that gives you? First, it gives you room to speculate with your hands. Second, it makes your foes nervous and edgy by forcing them to take their dubious holdings forward for twice what they wanted to pay. Third, it means your opponents will start checking to the raiser (you, the antifish), which will allow you to take a free card sometimes or bluff at the pot.

The circumstances aren't always right for antifish play, but if the circumstances *are* right and you don't seize the initiative, then you're just leaving money lying on the table. So do this: Look around for a game that's genial and reasonable—and then set out to render it senseless. Control is the issue, not profit. Although when an antifish takes control, profit is usually not far behind.

> *No kidding, next time you come into a new game,*
> *raise your own blind. Most people don't do it,*
> *and almost no one does it for strategic reasons. If*
> *nothing else, you get to feel what it's like*
> *to be fearless and bold.*

Are You Skeptical?

Frankly, I don't blame you. After all, I'm asking you to try a lot of odd strategies, and I'm protecting myself from your bad outcomes by glibly telling you that bad outcomes don't matter—that, in fact, the whole notion of outcomes is completely beside the point. I'm doing this for a reason. I'm doing it because I know this:

Good is the enemy of great.

If you play a fairly effective, modestly successful poker game, you have little enough incentive to throw it away for the uncertain promise of strategies that might be more successful but certainly seem dubious on their face. *Antifish? What the hell is an antifish? Why should I try to be one?* Because good is the enemy of the great, that's why. If you play a fairly effective, modestly successful poker game, and you're not willing to sacrifice the mind-set that informs such a game, then you have no hope of rising higher in your skills or achievement. You will, in short, be no better, ever, than you are right now.

So I suggest oddball strategies, and I encourage you to try them, not so much because I have faith in them (I do) but because I recognize this fundamental truth:

Change is growth.

If you're not willing to experience change, simply for the sake of change, then you can't expect to grow. The player you are now is the player you always will be.

That might be enough, except for one thing: The world of poker is dynamic. New players take up the game every day, and they take it up with an unbridled enthusiasm for book study, computer simulation, online play, and Internet chat. If you don't consistently sharpen your game, you'll be swiftly overtaken by those who do. I'd hate to see that happen to you. That's why I ask you to jump out of your comfort zone and into strange new realms. You have nothing to lose but some chips and some precious preconceived notions about how you approach the game. You might miss the chips, but the preconceived notions you can *definitely* do without.

DESCRIPTIVES

Below you will find some words that describe Killer Poker players, as I understand them to be. I'd like you to think about which words describe you. Be honest, please. Don't, for example, take credit for being patient if your idea of patience is waiting for the button to pass before you post into a new game. That's baseline patience, very ordinary stuff. You don't deserve extra credit for that. Truthfully now, would you say that you are:

> fearless, confident, bold, adventurous, unafraid, optimistic, opportunistic, dominant, relentless, ruthless, inventive, clever, self-aware, investigative, intuitive, observant, patient, articulate, intelligent, intense, far-sighted, devastating, merciless, humble, educated, tranquil, happy, strategic, daring, perplexing, unpredictable, analytical, overwhelming, well-equipped, exquisitely armed, clear-eyed, winning, sober, and high?

How, you may wonder, can a player be simultaneously sober and high? That's patently inconsistent, isn't it? Not necessarily, for when I say *high* in this context, I'm not talking about alcohol or drugs. I'm talking about spirit. *High* means entering the game enthusiastic, ready to go, and just flat thrilled at the prospect of destroying your foes. That's the kind of high I'm talking about—but you know that. You also know that a Killer Poker player is:

> organized, honest, introspective, committed, precise, targeted, focused, fit, energetic, healthy, well-rested, well-rounded, well-balanced, well-informed, dedicated, thorough, ethical, confident, arrogant, and loving.

Oh, loving? What's loving got to do with poker? I'll tell you what: If you are capable of love, you're also capable of self-awareness, and self-awareness is the rock upon which Killer Poker stands. If you don't have self-awareness, then just don't even bother to play, for your cause and your cash are already lost.

For instance, never again play a hand just for the hell of it. Why would you? Do you want to see what kind of damage you can do with that Q-8 suited? Well, plenty—to yourself. Now, if you're talking about attacking with a stealth holding that's one thing, but if you're just frisking around, just playing for fun or jest or just to see the flop, that's ridiculous. The Q-8 hand can be playable *if* you know why you're playing it and what you hope to accomplish. "Let's just see what happens" is a loser's philosophy, or no, not even a philosophy. It's a rationalization for unself-aware, self-destructive activity. You don't have time for that.

Look, Killer Poker is *hard*. It requires stamina, discipline, concentration, and a whole lot of other words that haven't even been coined yet. (Such as *beherenowedness;* Killer Poker requires that, too.) You have to train away your weakness and hone your strength. If you're watching a program on the TV above the dealer's head for even a single moment when you could be watching a hand unfold, then you're not taking your game seriously, and you're not playing Killer Poker.

How the mind wanders, though; how the mind does wander. Some boho calls for a new setup and that gives you a good 45 seconds to kill with nothing to do but watch the TV screen, so you do. No harm done, right? Who needs to concentrate on watching the dealer shuffle the cards? Then again, what if you get interested in the TV show? What if you miss the fact that the lady in seat three just borrowed a C-note from the gentleman sweating her play? You've lost out on an edge. What if you actually start to *care* whether Tiffany Biffany or Mameve Medwed wins the finals of the World Ice Dancing Competition? You might miss the fact that seat six is drinking double martinis. What if you start sneaking peeks at the screen during hands you're not in, or even ones you *are* in, while you're waiting for another player to act? How's your concentration now?

Poker is a slippery slope. A lapse in focus leads to a careless disregard for a downstream player's telegraphed intention to bet, resulting in a loose call, inaccurate calculation of pot odds, hunch play, dashed hope, and extravagant loss of chips. Do you want this? Of course not.

So give yourself some traction on the slope, some mental crampons, if you will. Give yourself a frank appraisal of the words that describe *you* as a poker player. Forget for a moment about the ideal discussed above. List what's *real* about the game you play. Don't be afraid of this evidence; it leads to a tougher, more capable you.

I'm not afraid of this evidence. I'll tell you everything I've been guilty of. Why, in the last week alone, I have been:

inattentive, impatient, hunchy, foolish, fragile,
frivolous, weak, loose, hesitant, passive, angry, flaky,
timid, tired, tilty, insecure, stressed, fearful,
transparent, illogical, reactive, apprehensive, hasty,
rash, distracted, stupid, lost, dazed, and confused.

Can you generate such a list? I'm not asking you to share it with me or anyone else, but I encourage you to share it with yourself, because every negative aspect of your game that you can identify is one you can start to eradicate. Open your eyes and see yourself as you are. Anything less will only impede your progress on the journey from the player you are to the player you want to be.

> *Just in the last week, what have you been? Don't tell me; tell your notebook.*

Out of Control

I'll tell you one thing I've never been at the poker table, not last week or any week, and that is *visibly enraged*. I've never thrown a card or cursed a dealer or berated a foe. I can't, in fact, imagine any set of circumstances that would find me raging against someone's bad play or my own bad luck. I find this sort of behavior not just abhorrent but incredibly self-destructive. Any time I see another player letting his anger get the best of him, I instantly know that this is a player I can beat.

Talk about a tell! The fool who throws cards at the dealer is demonstrating such a heavy emotional investment in outcome that he can't even contain his own fury. Someone who is that invested in outcome is clearly a player on tilt—not just in this moment but, functionally, all the time. At minimum this is a player more concerned with winning or losing money than with playing his best game. Beneath all this visible anger lies a deeper and more crucial reality: The player who rages in this manner has no self-awareness whatsoever.

It's manifest. If he had self-awareness, then he would recognize how these rank demonstrations of anger hurt his

game. If he had self-awareness, he would know that playing angry leaves him open to attack from more stable, less
emotional players. If he had the slightest shred of self-
awareness, he would recognize that this sort of ire is bad for
him, bad for the game, and bad for poker as a whole. If he
recognized any of this in himself, he would shut the "frick"
up and just get on with the game.

In fact it's astounding to me that the fury-heads last as
long in the game as they do. You would think that the first
episode of card hurling or, worse, card spindling would
warn a player that he is *badly out of control.* Strangely, this
doesn't happen. I suppose that if your hostility is that high
and your rage is that raw, it's easy to direct all of your emo-
tions outward and *blame the universe* for something that is,
let's face it, completely and entirely your own fault. Our
responsibility as Killer Poker players is simple and twofold:
First, identify these players and exploit the crap out of
them; and second, never be this kind of player, not even
for an instant.

Unless you're faking it.

Unless you have decided that there's an image play to
be made by railing against the cosmic forces that seem to
oppress you so. I would validate this strategy as long as you
stopped short of tearing up cards or abusing dealers or other
players. Even in the name of image, and even if the strategy
is fundamentally sound, some things are just over the line.

Then again, some things just aren't. Things like being a
bully.

BULLY

Are you a bully by nature? Probably not. Probably you
weren't the sort of child who waylaid other kids on their
way to school and extorted their lunch money. That sort of

person generally doesn't grow up to be a poker player. No, that sort of person grows up to do 20-to-life for aggravated manslaughter. So you might not have a bully's nature to begin with. The question, then, is this: Can you acquire bully consciousness? Can you develop the aggressiveness, the meanness, and the perverse desire to destroy that it takes to succeed in the competitive, Darwinian schoolyard that we call poker?

I think you can. I think you can train yourself to disregard your own fear while simultaneously inspiring fear in others. I'm not saying you need to be *rude*—just forceful, but *very forceful*.

Bullying Short Money

So let's paint a picture. You're playing at a limit where you feel comfortable. For the sake of discussion, we'll say $6–$12. A typical buy-in for a game at this limit is $200, one rack of $2 chips. You notice someone sitting down and buying in for just $60. This should make your eyes light up because short money is *always* a target for bully behavior. Fierce Killer Poker player that you are, you start to plan your attack.

Before we get to that attack, though, let's contemplate short money for a moment. Why do we believe that short money is, in fact, a target of opportunity for the Killer Poker bully? Off the top of my head, I can think of three reasons.

1. Short money may be scared money. Many players down on their luck or down on their bankroll will buy in short hoping to score quickly and play with your money for the rest of the session.
2. Short money may be loser's money. Many players try to slow down a losing jag by minimizing their

buy-ins. Even though a player is new to your game, he may have been playing—and losing—at another table for hours.

3. Short money is always vulnerable to negative fluctuation. Even in the hands of a superior player, a short stack can be swallowed up by one or two bad beats. Thus a player with short money must often play tighter than he should, just to protect his short stack.

Meanwhile, back in bully-land, you have noticed a player buying in short, for whatever reason, and you wonder now how to proceed. The answer is simple: *fists first!*

Raise this player the very first chance you get. If he posts behind the button, raise on that. Raise if he limps in. Raise as soon as you can, especially if your raise gives you a chance to get heads-up or close to heads-up against the short money player. Raise!

Raise, raise, raise, raise, raise! And don't care what your cards are! Why should you care what your cards are? You have your foe's fearful state of mind and lack of ammo on your side. That, plus your bully tactics, gives you plenty of edge.

In other words, who need cards? It's not you, not in this circumstance. All you need is chips, because your poor foe forgot to have enough.

Sixty dollars is a pitifully small amount to bring into a $6–$12 game. His sixty bucks will give him a look at just ten unraised flops, and that's hardly enough to overcome even normal fluctuation in poker. If you *raise* anytime this player enters a pot, you can cut his looks in half. At that point, the mathematics of poker will simply overwhelm his short stack. He can't outplay you—he lacks the ammunition—so he'll have to catch very lucky in order to survive your determined assault on his stack.

Remember that this is a player who's running scared or running bad to begin with. Even if he is neither frightened nor tilty, he desperately needs to play in unraised pots, because his only hope of parlaying his short buy-in into a decent win is to hit some hands right away. When you make him double his pre-flop investment on every hand, you take away his only viable strategy.

Are you worried about letting him "get well" at your expense? Don't worry! Especially don't worry if he's playing a blind hand. His blind hand is a random hand. It's more likely to be rags than riches. Even if he's in the pot with something he considers true value, the flop still has to hit his hand in order for him to feel good about going forward—something that your ongoing pressure will make him reluctant to do.

He's in a real quandary, this short stack. Because he's under-funded, he feels like he has to play tight and wait for premium hands. But because he's under-funded, the blinds and collection cost him more, relatively speaking, than they cost anyone else. The longer he waits for premium hands, the closer he gets to broke. So he'll limp with speculative holdings like J-T, and hope the flop hits him hard. *Make him pay!* Raise into him, knowing that every time you do, you push him (yes, that's right, *bully* him) into situations where his level of discomfort is jacked up even higher.

This is the application of Killer Poker to a certain class of player: the short-stacker. Whenever you see them, hit them and hit them hard! Never give them a chance to put their safe little strategy to work.

Once in a while you'll fail. Once in a while they'll draw out on you. Once in a while they'll catch good cards and trap you. That doesn't change the fact that they started out short-stacked, and that's still a hole that they have to climb out of to get on an equal footing with you. Remember that they can only win with superior cards, while you can win with *any cards at all.*

> **Buying in short is one of the worst things you can do in poker. When you see someone doing it, attack *those short stacks*. Make them pay for their mistake.**

Learning Curves

For a lot of players, this notion of "winning with any cards at all" represents a real watershed in their thinking. Once they learn that, in many situations, the act of betting matters much more than the cards they hold, they undergo a paradigm shift, and leave their old style of play behind. To put it another way: When you stop playing the cards and start playing the players, you see your game in a whole new light.

This raises a larger issue of learning as it relates to poker, the issue of *learning curves,* and specifically the issue of what to do when the curves flatten out.

When you're learning something new, anything new, your learning curve is quite steep. Since the subject at hand is largely unknown to you, you can acquire a lot of new, useful information in a short time with little effort. After a while, and after a period of aggressive learning, it becomes harder to acquire new information for the simple reason that there's less genuinely new information lying around. Instead of being on a learning curve, you find yourself on a *learning plateau.*

Now, there's good news and bad news about being on a plateau. The good news is that you're at a higher level than you were before. The bad news is that you're no longer going up. It was easy to learn when information was plentiful. It gets harder to learn when information is scarce.

This is why so many players tend to reach a certain betting limit and move no higher. Having fairly well conquered, for example, the realm of $6–$12 to $9–$18 poker, many players never seem to make the jump from there to $15–$30, $20–$40 and beyond. Why? They stopped learning. They acquired enough information to beat the game they're playing and didn't bother to acquire any more. They became satisfied with their plateau, and there they sit to this day.

Does this make them unhappy? No. Are they bad people? Not necessarily. We might accuse them of being lazy, but maybe they're just content. They're playing the kind of poker they want to play at a limit where they feel comfortable.

As a Killer Poker player, you won't be satisfied with that. You want to conquer this limit, the one above this limit, the one above that, and so on. But there's a problem. The problem is you do reach plateaus, and you do get stuck. How does one get off the plateau and move up onto the next learning curve?

The answer, curiously, is not to go higher but rather to go deeper. Deeper within, to the place where lies your root understanding not just of poker but of your true self.

> *To open your mind to new learning, you first must*
> **open your mind.**

This is why so many players become complacent and really stop growing in their game. They don't want to open their minds. They are, in a very real sense, afraid to look within. They find it daunting, threatening, maybe even impossible to face certain hard truths about themselves.

In the next section, I'll raise the question of when and whether it's appropriate *not to play poker at all*. This is a question that many poker players simply can't address.

They operate on the assumption that it's always right to play poker and that they're never off their game. It's an absurd assumption, of course, but one that habitual players make every day. They don't want to challenge the assumption and they wouldn't have the self-awareness and honesty to challenge it even if they wanted to.

So they stop growing and they stop learning; not because it has become hard to acquire new information. Goodness knows there's no shortage of new information. They stop learning because it has become hard to apply a new honesty to themselves, and without that honesty, deeper understanding of the game becomes impossible.

4

♣♠♦♥

THE POKER SELF

♣♠♦♡

PASS!

Do you ever *not* play poker? Do you ever put on your hat and coat to go play, but then change your mind? Maybe you even get down the driveway. Maybe you get halfway to the freeway, when suddenly, confronted by the prospect of enduring an hour in traffic just for the enjoyment of playing poker—an enjoyment you don't even feel that much like enjoying right now—you just put the brakes on the whole proposition and head back home. If you do, you're in tune with the little tiny voice inside you that says, "Pass!" It's a good voice to listen to.

You were up a little late last night. Maybe had a drink or two. Didn't get a good night's sleep. Are you feeling a little light in the wallet? Don't feel a hundred percent? *Pass!*

Still getting over a cold, as that wad of tissue in your pocket attests? *Pass!* Spewing aerosol mayhem over all your fellow players does no one any favors.

You got killed the last time you played, and now you're bent on revenge against the world. Look at you! You're playing angry and you haven't even started playing yet. *Pass!*

Your spouse doesn't think you play too much poker, but you think she thinks you do. So maybe spend a little quality time with her. *Pass!*

Got other work to do? *Pass!* Don't feel sharp? *Pass!* Just had a big meal? *Pass!* Forcing a short session? *Pass!* Just don't have the bucks? *Pass!*

Can it be that you never pass? Do you go play poker no matter what physical, mental, or financial shape you're in? Knowing when *not* to play poker is crucial. Everyone talks table selection, but sometimes the best table to choose is *(d) none of the above.* When your frame of body or frame of mind deny you the possibility of playing your best, *you must not play!*

But many players play anyway. They quash the little tiny voice inside that says *pass,* and therefore enter the card room under falsest of pretexts: "Even though I don't really feel like playing, I feel like I can still play well. Probably I'll just play for a short spell and then go home." *Go home broke that is.*

Well, what made them go play in the first place? What drive or desire overrode their own best interest? Why did they put themselves at risk? God knows there are plenty of excuses for playing poker. Ever used one of these?

- I'm a professional, I've got to put in my hours.
- I've been working hard at my job and now I deserve a break.
- I need some extra cash.
- I think my luck is turning.
- I'm bored or I've got nothing better to do or both.
- It's right on my way to wherever.
- My spouse is traveling, and while the cat's away the mice will play.

- It's a holiday (or payday or graveyard shift) and I can't pass up all the loose money I just *know is* out there.

What reasons do you give yourself? How does your nefarious urge override your judgment? It's not a crucial question or anything; it's just a matter of how honest you're willing to be with yourself, and how hard you'll work to reveal that honesty. Oh, oh, sorry—you don't want to work on your game? Then thanks; *I'll take your money now.*

Anyway, the fact is you don't fail to work on your game because you're lazy, you fail to work on your game because you're scared. Scared to confront yourself.

Confronting yourself; writing it down: That's the real hard work. If you write it down, you own it. There's no hiding from the truth in black and white, and some people would rather just pretend that that truth doesn't exist. Okay, that's okay. They don't want to take responsibility for their poker, but *you* do, don't you? So ask yourself: Why do you play in the first place?

- To make money.
- To have fun.
- For companionship.
- For competition.
- For the comps and coffee.
- To test myself.
- To kill time.
- For the buzz.
- It's a place where I can relax.
- It's a place where I can shine.
- It's a place where I can hide.

Or what else? *What else?* If you're going to play poker, the least you can do is know why. *Really* know why. Don't tell me you've already thought about it, because you haven't, not deeply and meaningfully, not until you've also written it down.

Forgive me for beating this dead horse, but you don't have to be *any kind of writer* in order to write about your poker. Just simply record the facts inside your head. Just simply generate the articulate honesty that helps you get a grip on your game. That shouldn't be so tough. Does any of this sound like you?

> Sometimes I play for the rush. Dragging big pots is big fun. So is the sense of confidence and dominance I get from playing Killer Poker. I play because I seek—lust after—that moment when I know, just *know*, that no one at the table can touch me.

Perhaps you find yourself thinking, "Why do I have to write it down? Can't I just muse upon it in the car while I'm driving to the club? Won't that be sufficient?" Perhaps. But is the radio on? Are you talking on your cell phone? You can't devote just part of your brain to poker. You have to devote all of it, or the job does not get done.

Write it down! Taking notes on your poker is guaranteed to focus your thinking. Again, I'm not talking about novels, just simple observations about who you are and how you are when you play. For example:

> At my best, I am super aggressive, and super tuned-in. The patterns of others' bets speak to me, and my clearest, strongest game responds.

> At my worst, I call too much, and call down players whom I devoutly wish to catch bluffing but who I know, in my heart, are just not.

> I frequently discount position, counting on my playing ability (or native intelligence or boyish good looks) to overcome that disadvantage.

For further example—well, you tell me. Take notes on
your play: little stories on what you do right and what you
do wrong. And don't forget to *pass* from time to time, for
sometimes the poker you don't play is the most profitable
Killer Poker of all.

> *The difference between hobby and habit: Hobby
> you do 'cause you want to; habit you do
> 'cause you have to. Next time you go to play
> poker—don't! Do something else instead.
> Prove to yourself that your interest in poker
> is a hobby, not a habit.*

Beating a Dead Horse

You might think I am truly flogging the dead equine with
all this noise about notes and notebooks and serious introspection. I might even agree with you. I certainly am bela-
boring the point. So I find myself wondering *why?* What do
I think is so important about these notes and notebooks
and serious introspection? I think it's this: The world of
public poker has become so competitive that you have to
deal yourself some kind of edge. Talking to yourself, articu-
lating the facts of your play to the only person who needs
that information, is one reliable way to get that edge.

Look, we all have access to the same information. We've
all read the same books on strategy and tactics. We visit the
same websites and chat in the same chatrooms. There are
no secrets anymore. So it comes to pass that when we sit
down to do battle with other well-informed players we find
ourselves, for all intents and purposes, equally armed. At
that point the only thing that makes a difference is *how well
each of us uses the weapons we all share.* I believe, and I'm
doing my best to convince you, that awareness and detailed
honesty give you better control of the weapons we all share.

That's why I encourage you to develop a certain schizophrenia: the trick of playing your game of poker and, at the same time, watching yourself play your game. Spy on yourself, so to speak, and then report back on what you find. It's a priceless investigation.

ICTAFCOA

ICTAFCOA is an acronym that stands for *Increasing Commitment To A Failing Course Of Action*. It's a terribly powerful concept in poker because it explains so well how we go so wrong.

You're playing Omaha/8, and you pick up a big drawing low like A-2-3-4. Against a table full of Cally Wallies, you feel justified in making a raise, and so you do. Nothing wrong with that; at this point a raise is a rising course of action. However, when the flop comes T-9-8 in suits you don't own, your course of action turns and runs downhill. Sure you still have a chance (about 24 percent) of catching two cards to a low, but unless there's a table full of players chasing high, your expectation is negative—your course of action is failing. Yet you call anyway!

This is the textbook definition of increasing commitment to a failing course of action: When you keep trying the same thing over and over again, long past any reasonable hope of achieving your goal.

Say you're heads up against a single Wally. You have tried to bluff him off his hand for five straight hands now, and he's called you down every time. At some point you become convinced that he *can't possibly call again*. So you bet. He calls—and he wins. ICTAFCOA—*increasing commitment to a failing course of action*.

You're in a game that's way too tough for you and you've already been pushed around on a bunch of hands.

Instead of trading down to an easier game, you stubbornly stick to your game plan (such as it is) of call and pray, call and pray, call and pray. Again, ICTAFCOA. Unless you catch *very* lucky, or come to your senses in time, you must surely go broke in the game.

Flopheads have an increasing commitment to a failing course of action. They just can't stop believing that *this* time the flop will hit their 8-3 offsuit.

People who call with pocket kings in the face of an ace on the flop and multi-way raises have ICTAFCOA. They feel that their pocket kings deserve a better fate than that.

Compulsive gamblers who gamble further, in the dark hope of getting well or getting even, are caught in the worst throes of this affliction. Enough said.

No, *not* enough said! Because you're not a compulsive gambler. You're a conscious, conscientious Killer Poker player. You know what you're doing and give your best effort when you play. There are holes in your game, though, and if you're not *forever* trying to plug those holes, then ICTAFCOA has you by the throat, at least a little.

There is a way out. There is. Because it's a fascinating thing about ICTAFCOA: People trapped in this maelstrom will try the same solution over and over and over again until—suddenly and happily—they become convinced that the solution *will not work*. In that moment, they experience a revelation and then, almost miraculously, they see a solution that *will* work.

Here's an example from the real world. Poor Joe is trying to tighten a bolt. Simple thing, tightening a bolt, but Poor Joe doesn't happen to have the right wrench in his hand. No, he has that pair of pliers he grabbed from the tool drawer in the kitchen because he thinks it's the only appropriate tool he owns. So he tries and tries and tries to tighten the bolt, but the stubborn bolt won't tighten. The pliers just can't do the job. Finally, Poor Joe *gives up* on the damn pliers, and in that instant he suddenly remembers the set of socket wrenches he has out in the garage. Probably he knew they were there all along, but while he still entertained hope that the pliers would work, he blocked the wrenches from his mind. Now that he's convinced that the pliers never will work, he gets the proper tool and completes his task.

That's the real world. In the real world, we flow through this blunder-and-revelation cycle over and over again. In poker, you can skip the frustrating blunder stage. You don't have to repeat the failing course of action.

- You can *stop* trying to bluff the unbluffable.
- You can *stop* trying to bully the bully-proof.
- You can *stop* letting your same old errors bleed your bankroll.
- You can *stop* doing these other five things:

1. _____
2. _____
3. _____
4. _____
5. _____

You can *recognize* your natural commitment to failing courses of action and *change course now!*

More than anything, this means opening your eyes to the actual reality of the way you play. Do you find yourself folding when you should call because you're not sure if the odds justify a call? Then *study* the stupid odds so that next time you'll know. Do you call when you should raise because congenital timidity stunts your game? Then *study* your timidity, and discover its roots in your fear of losing lots of money. Recognize that quashing the fear of losing lots of money is the straight and well-lit path to winning lots of money instead.

I could go on. I could give you a dozen more examples of how stubborn refusal to surrender a flawed paradigm keeps people from discovering the paradigm that actually works. I could, but I won't, because the only flaws that matter are the flaws that *you* have in *your* play. No one knows those flaws better than you. So go to work! Tear yourself free from increasing commitments to failing courses of action. ICTAFCOA may keep Poor Joe from tightening a bolt, but it need not keep you from fixing your game.

> *Buying more chips when you're losing—hemorrhaging at the wallet, as it's called—is the biggest ICTAFCOA of all. It's okay to rebuy if you're temporarily behind in an otherwise good game, but that's not why most people do it. Spot the ICTAFCOA players in your game. Know them by their reflexive rebuys. They'll be your primary revenue streams over time.*

Revelation

When we encounter new ideas in poker, they often strike us with the force of revelation. There are two things worth noting about revelation. One is that it's the nature of revelation to propel us through the paradigm shift, to change the way we think. The other is that it's the nature of revelation to *fade,* and unless we keep refreshing our thinking with new revelations—even revelations that illuminate the exact same idea—we become stale in our thinking and habituated in our play. A concept that once lent great clarity to our game eventually becomes only a *memory* of that concept, and its usefulness weakens accordingly. That's how

revelation works: One day you're Paul on the road to Da-
mascus and the next day you're just looking at slides from
the trip.

Consider this: You come across a concept like the *any-
ace line*. This line divides hold'em games into two types,
those where they'll generally play any ace with any kicker,
and those where they generally need high kickers to compete. Powered by the force of this concept, you resolve not
to sink beneath the any-ace line. You vow to play only good
aces, especially in games where the play of bad aces runs
rampant. That works for a while, but eventually you forget
what got you so excited about being tight with your aces.
You see (or think you see) weak aces holding up and winning big pots. You see (or think you see) suited aces flopping nut flushes all the time. You forget all the times your
weak aces got outkicked. The power of the concept starts to
fade. You go back to doing what you were doing before,
and your game suffers as a result.

Now here comes a new concept, *little poison*. It instructs
you that little cards are poison in hold'em and that their
poison can contaminate other cards, even aces. Armed with
this information, you once more tighten up your play of
aces, and once more your performance improves—until the
revelation fades. Then you have to go find a whole new
revelation to energize your awareness of, and commitment
to, correct play once again.

This reminds me of a joke:

"How many naked virgins does it take to change a light
bulb?"
"How many ya got?"

So then the question is, "How many different ways are
there to say 'don't play weak aces,' or anything else useful
in poker?" And the answer is the same: "How many ya
got?"

> *One way to make sure you don't get promiscuous
> with aces is to record your play of them. You'll
> soon find that you'd rather dump a bad ace than
> try justifying to yourself why you thought it was
> a good idea to call.*

MISTAKIES

Did you notice that I mispelled "mistakes"? My copy editor
did, and corrected it three times before I finally persuaded
her that I spelled it that way on purpose. Did you notice
that I misspelled "misspelled"? My copy editor missed that
one, which proves that even professionals can fall victim to
confirmation bias. You see what you expect to see, be it a
word spelled a certain way or a bad river card that proves
once again how damned unlucky we are.

A screenwriter friend of mine insists that there's a con-
spiracy among screenwriters to use the number 23 in all
movies. He says that the number 23 has mystic significance,
and if you just look for it, you'll see how they (the cabal of
screenwriters) use the number 23 when any other number
would do just as well. Do you know what? It's true: If you
look for the number 23, or any number, you'll see it much
more often than if you don't look for it. Just like you'll see
a word spelled correctly (or a flop fall unfavorably) if you
expect it to be so. But I'm not here to wax mystic on the
esoteric significance of the number 23. I'm here to contemplate the nature of mistakes. That's why I misspelled the
word: to draw your attention to it, and to get you to medi-
tate on the nature of mistakes, and the nature of your own.

Think about your last session. Did you play perfectly?
No? Well, good for you for admitting your shortcomings.
This shows that you're playing clear-eyed, honest poker.
You're not pretending that you're perfect, which is such a

useless pretense anyhow, because, hey, nobody is. Now do me a favor. Take a moment and list some of the mistakes you made. You may have listed some of these before. That's okay. Go right ahead and list them again. That's how they get fixed in your mind, and ultimately fixed in your game.

Poker is best played with aggressiveness, this we know—but a little humility helps too. When you admit your mistakes, you cause yourself a modest amount of psychic pain, but you gain a deeper understanding of yourself in the context of your play, and that saves you money—oh, just lots and lots of money—in the end.

So, again, what are your most recent mistakes? No kidding, write them down. Here, I'll even give you some space:

Mistakie: _____

Mistakie: _____

Mistakie: _____

Mistakie: _____

Mistakie: _____

Okay, though that's you being honest and clearing the cobwebs out of your play, that's only half the battle. In addition to the mistakes you recognize, there's a whole bunch that just pass by unseen. This presents us with a familiar Zen conundrum: How can you see what you can't see?

For starters, *question everything.* Challenge your assumptions every time you play. (Don't assume that a word is spelled correctly just because you trust the speller.) Study your patterns and habits. Ask yourself: *Do I do this because it makes sense, or do I do it because it's what I do?*

Take A-2 in Omaha/8. Some people raise every time with those cards. Are they right to do so? Maybe, depending on the texture of the game, but I'm willing to bet that these reflex-raisers aren't thinking about the texture of the game. They see that A-2 and *bam!* They're in there raising. They don't know if this is correct play or not. How can they? They never question the action. Likewise, you'll find people who never raise with A-2 and never question that it's right to do so. They can't both be right, right?

Hard and fast rules just hold you hard and fast. Look, A-2 is a drawing hand. You want lots of players in the pot. So if you're in early position, you don't want to raise with this hand and knock players out. If you're around back and seven players have already jumped in, then you can raise to build a pot. It's not correct to *always* raise with A-2. It's not correct to *never* raise with A-2. It's not correct to *always* or *never* do anything.

So, have confidence in your ability, but also have doubt about your actions. Constantly seek to deepen your understanding of why you do what you do, and challenge those underlying assumptions, even the ones you trust. The only way you can improve your play is to take stuff that doesn't work and replace it with stuff that does work, and then take stuff that works and replace it with stuff that works better.

Somewhere, for instance, back in the dim and distant past, you came across a guide to starting hands in seven-card stud. You learned a useful shorthand of *three-straight, three-flush, big pairs, live cards, and trips.* You learned to stay away from problematic holdings like naked aces that tempted you to bluff too much and represented muscle you didn't have. Then later, once you built up a little shrewdness and confidence, you started pushing those naked aces because you convinced yourself that you were shrewd and confident enough to get away from the hand at a modest cost if things didn't go your way.

You may have been right, but if you were wrong it cost you a lot of money, and you never knew because you never tested the assumption.

A junk hand is a junk hand is a junk hand, but you

won't recognize it as such unless you keep your mind open to the possibility that mistakes have crept into your play. If you confuse a premium hand with a junk hand, you're making a mistake that you don't even see. That way lies madness, or if not madness, then at least poverty.

So I invite you to invite a little psychic pain into your play. It's one (good) thing to admit obvious mistakes, but it's something altogether else to look for and ferret out and destroy all the hidden ones. Do this. I promise it won't be a mistakie.

> *If you're going to play junk, at least* **admit** *it's junk. Tell yourself, "I know I shouldn't be playing this hand but I am." That's orders of magnitude better than never admitting you knew it was junk in the first place.*

It's All About Poker

Sometimes I forget which book I'm writing. When the subject matter veers off into confirmation bias or the inexplicable presence of the number 23, I worry that I've lost focus and stopped writing about poker. Then I remember that it's *all* about poker. There is nothing—*nothing*—in our daily human experience that can't illuminate and instruct our poker play if we let it.

Hell, even being stuck in traffic can do that.

Where I come from, we describe a certain type of driver as a "fast mover." This is someone who disregards both safety and courtesy as he jumps from lane to lane in an effort *to get where he's going sooner.* We have another name for this type of driver. It's rude and I won't print it here, but I'll give you a hint, it rhymes with duckface. The point is, there are fast movers in poker too, players who are congenitally tilted by their own impatience. When you see fast movers on the freeway let it remind you to look for fast movers at the casino, because fast movers on the freeway are a hazard, but fast movers in poker are a target of opportunity for you.

Is it true, JV? Really? That everything relates to poker, resonates of poker, and informs and enlightens the play of poker? What about, uhm, this coffee cup here in my hand? How does that sharpen my game?

Well, you tell me. Tell me three useful tips for poker that you can extract from the humble coffee cup? Tell me yours, then I'll tell you mine.

1. _____
2. _____
3. _____

1. Don't drink too much coffee. If you have reached the point where your concentration must be artificially fueled, it's time to call it a night.
2. Look around the table and be aware of who's ordering coffee, or food, or anything else. In the moments when their attention is centered on *getting served,* that's attention they've taken away from the game. In those moments they're a little vulnerable, and you should be more likely to attack.
3. Caffeine is addictive, yes it is. It's a relatively benign addiction and doesn't skew our play too much. What other addictions swirl around a poker game? Who among your opponents is addicted, and to what? Do you have nicotine junkies? Beer pounders? Is that young guy in the mirrored shades sneaking off to get high? Who's hooked on playing? Who's hooked on losing?

It's amazing what you can learn from just coffee.

One thing I notice when I'm writing a novel or a screen-play is how everything in the real world seems to connect to the world of my story. When I'm in that state of mind, I write much more effectively. The same is true of poker. When you're in the frame of mind where *everything* in your world seems to connect with your poker, your poker must improve. Why? Simply because you're alive in your mind, and thinking about your game in new and different ways all the time. So seek these connections—force them if you have to—for the player who thinks about poker in every context has an edge over those who think about it only at the table.

NONSENSE

Many is the time I've raked a pot while saying, "They can't figure out your strategy if you don't have one." The percep-tion of nonsense is a strength of my game.

Note that I said *perception* of nonsense. There's a differ-ence between real nonsense and perceived nonsense, a cru-cial distinction. It's real nonsense, clearly, to cold-call three bets before the flop with 6-4 offsuit. It's only *perceived* non-sense to take that same hand and open for a raise on the button with (to your keen eye) proven willing-to-surrender blinds waiting to act behind. From that raise can come two good outcomes. First, the blinds might fold either right then or under subsequent bluffing pressure. Second, you could hit the flop, drive all the way, and get the chance to show down your winning rags—your perceived nonsense—whereupon you get to say, "They can't figure out your strat-egy if you don't have one," while you stack the chips.

So, how can 6-4 offsuit not be worth a call but yet be worth a raise? The answer lies not in the cards, but in the situation surrounding the cards. If you call three bets with a bad hand, you have scant chance of winning and no chance of enhancing your image. If you raise with bad cards, you put yourself in a position to do both. To me that's *enlightened nonsense,* and I encourage you to look for opportunities to thrust it upon your foes.

The trouble is, some of your foes aren't that smart. They don't appreciate the distinction between real nonsense and perceived nonsense. In other words, they truly don't have a strategy (nay, nor even a clue) and you have to adjust accordingly. You've heard this set of adjustments boiled down to such trite-and-truisms as, "Don't waste money advertising to players who aren't paying attention," and, "Don't bluff into the bluff-proof." This is wise wisdom, but it only goes so far. Forget about tweaking your tactics; you must tweak your entire approach.

Isn't it true where you play, for example, that almost any player who enters the pot pre-flop for a single bet will stick around in the face of a raise? They may (or may not) have been right to make the first call but they rarely stop to contemplate whether it's correct or not to call a reraise or even two.

Think about it: Rare is the time that you see a player jump in for a single bet and then, in the face of subsequent pre-flop heat say, "Whoa, I really have no business in this pot after all." As a consequence, we see some pretty funky holdings in some fairly hefty pots. At which point, of course, it becomes correct to call with thin draws, and sensible players take some vile and horrendous beats at the hands of the woodentops around them—woodentops who then get to say, and unfortunately mean, "They can't figure out your strategy if you don't have one."

You have to adjust your approach. If you know that opponents will make bad calls on top of other bad calls, then you can't consistently raise to thin the field, because the field won't thin. All your raise does is give them a chance to compound their errors. That's not a bad thing, but recognize that in this sort of game any pre-flop raise you make into previous callers will probably just increase the chance that you're going to have to show down the best hand in order to claim the pot. Thus, you want to drive even harder with big tickets but back off your raises with drawing hands like suited connectors and middle pairs, where—at least in this sort of game—your equity develops *after* you've hit your draw.

The thing about true believers is *they always call*. In the long run, we know, these muttonchops are doomed to lose. So just keep hammering away with your quality cards, avoid mixing it up with trash, and know that eventually all their loose calls will come back to haunt them. In the meantime, it's the short run and not the long run, and it's vital that you remain clear in your mind about the difference between real and perceived nonsense; between sinking to their level and only *seeming* to sink.

In most low-limit games, and even a surprising number of those at middle limits, you will witness almost flabbergasting mistakes hand after hand, hour after hour, day after day. You can beat these games, but it requires sensitivity to real nonsense, and a willingness to project perceived nonsense, on your part. Keep your wits about you while simultaneously seeming to lose your mind. Make strong plays against weak opponents while talking quite a lot about your purportedly weak plays against superior foes. Punish them for their mistakes while appearing to be making mistakes of your own. In other words, play your strength and advertise your weakness. They can't figure out your strategy if you don't have one—and if you play your cards right, they'll never know that you do.

How do you know if you're playing in a nonsense game? Try raising into a large field in late position pre-flop and see if anyone folds. When they don't—and they won't—you'll know that your profit must come from pressing your big hands and not trying to get too cute.

Hit to Win

Let's talk about the *hit-to-win* game, a very common game style in the low- to mid-limit universe of card room poker. Hit-to-win, as the name implies, means that you're going to have to hit your hand to win the pot. This is different from big bet poker where the right move at the right time wins the pot regardless of the cards you hold.

In a typical hit-to-win hold'em game, on any given deal you might face active participants with as wide a range of holdings as: K♣ Q♥; 8-8; 6♦ 5♦; A-x; J-T; or Q♣ 9♣. Even if you've got a good hand, say pocket jacks, most flops will give someone a better hand or a better draw than yours. When you're playing in the hit-to-win milieu, how can you put anyone on a hand? Does a flop of 7-6-3 *help* someone? It could—if they're in there with 5-4 suited—and they could very well be in there with just that hand!

So how do you protect yourself? Do you raise with your pocket jacks to thin the field? Well, you can try—but if 6♦ 5♦ is already in the pot for one bet, he'll sure stick around for two. Then if he hits only part of the flop, he'll have (or imagine he has) odds to call any long shot the flop happens to offer. Plus, if you raise with jacks, what will you do with a flop that contains any A, K, or Q? You can't be confident betting on the flop, not against hit-to-winners who could be in there with any naked A, K, or Q.

This is truly the double-edge sword of hit-to-win. When

your opponents make loose calls, they take away the muscle of your raise. On the other hand, when they make loose calls, they are *playing incorrectly*, which is exactly what you want them to do. In a very real sense they're forcing you to play their game, not yours. Some of your aggressive moves are neutralized, and many of your bluff attempts become futile. What you're left with is your own modified version of hit-to-win, where you, like they, are hoping to connect with the flop in a major way.

The big difference is this: You start with good cards; they start with anything. I want to repeat this, because it's so important: They start with *anything,* but you start with *good cards*. So even if you're playing hit-to-win, you have a head start over the field. Over time—and it will *take* time—that head start will redound to your profit.

Remember: Just because your opponents are playing incorrectly doesn't mean that you can too. Otherwise you're all playing the same brainless game of hit-to-win, and what kind of edge do you have then?

In a very loose game in which most players see the flop and most hands are called down on the river, your edge comes simply from playing quality cards and playing aggressively when you hit. This is not the type of game for semi-bluffs and steals. It doesn't mean you're not playing Killer Poker. Killer Poker is adaptive; in this game, Killer Poker means playing good cards, punishing the Wallies when you make a hand, and not trying to buy any pots from opponents who think folding is something you only do with laundry.

SORROW—A REFLECTION

You got hammered again last night and now you're feeling sorry for yourself. Sorrow, as we know, is an emotion you can't afford, thanks to a little thing called self-fulfilling prophecy: The sorrier you feel for yourself, the sorrier you'll play—but let's see how it happened anyhow.

You raised before the flop with pocket aces, just like you knew you should. So far so good, but you got three callers, which is about two callers more than you'd like. Immediately you started to anticipate disaster. Why? Just 'cause; just 'cause those darned aces *never* hold up for you; and just 'cause there's no justice.

Well, the flop comes J-6-2, and you bet right out. Right on! No one could have called your pre-flop raise with a J-6 or 6-2, could they? *Could they?* Well, sure they could, if they're bad weak players bent on punishing noble-and-long-suffering you, but let's let that go for now. Let's pretend that only reasonable people with reasonable hands can call your raise pre-flop and also your bet on the flop. What's a reasonable hand in this situation? Top pair with a good kicker? How good is that hand against a pair of aces? Let's count the outs.

Assuming that your hand doesn't improve, any jack gets that hand home, plus any card that hits the kicker. So your foe with the good hand has five outs to beat you. With two cards to come, he's no worse than 5-1 against improving. His call on the flop throws one bet into a pot already containing at least nine bets (four pre-flop calls for two bets, plus your bet on the flop). Of course, if the board pairs he's going to need a jack to beat you, but he'll only factor that in if he puts you on an overpair to the board, which he might not do, not in a loose, nose-open game like this. Nor will he consider that, if his kicker is an ace, he's dead to the aces in your hand. So his call, no matter how much you personally hate, loathe, and despise it, makes some kind of sense to him.

The turn brings a brick and you're happy. I don't need

to remind you that happy and sad have no place in Killer Poker, but you're happy just the same, and who can blame you? You're one card away from having your aces hold up. So you bet. Why not? What else would you do? You're one card away from happiness. You bet. He calls without hesitation.

Then the dreaded jack comes on the river—and you bet. *Why would you do that?* Because you have convinced yourself that your opponent is *not* on exactly the hand he *must* be on in order to call on the flop and call again on the turn. Do you credit your enemies with *no* brains? That's wishful thinking, not Killer Poker. Play the hand that's being played, not the hand you wish for!

You're sad that your foe caught a jack to beat you, but when you reconstruct the hand, you realize that he wasn't that far out of line. It turns out that he had J-Q, and who wouldn't expect J-Q to call just one more bet before the flop in a loose, nose-open game like this? You've said it yourself many times—it's your chief lament about this game—*they call anything with anything around here*. So why should you be surprised when a reasonable hand called a reasonable raise? Answer: You shouldn't. You shouldn't be surprised at all.

Even if your foe was wrong to call before the flop—and he wasn't, not by his standards, and not by the standards of many people you play against—he wasn't wrong to call after the flop, not if you had the hand he put you on. Maybe he even played it too weakly. Maybe he should have raised. Or maybe he just figured that you'd do his job for him—and lo and behold, you did! Once he called the flop, he was committed to the river, unless an overcard came and scared him off. An overcard didn't come. He won; you lost. So what?

Maybe you think his analysis is all wet. After all, doing

a quick count of your own outs—all those aces and pair cards—you could conclude that you had him totally out-outed. Maybe you did, but your analysis only holds up from his point of view if he has put you on an overpair. Most of the time, especially in this game, a raiser in your position has overcards, not overpairs. He put you on A-K or A-Q and thought he had the best hand.

You think that's unfair. Hmm, I don't recall seeing the words *life is fair* printed on the contract, but what's *really* unfair is what you then turned around and did to yourself.

When your aces got cracked, you dropped into the well of sadness and lost control of your game. You figured that if some gonzo-bonzo bonehead can crack your aces with Q-J, then you should be able to make *any* hand stand up, including the 3-2 you were dealt next. So instead of folding, you called. Only you're a Killer Poker player, so instead of calling, you raised. As I often say, I never hate a raise, but in this case, well, not to put too terribly fine a point on it—*are you nuts?* Weren't you watching? You just had aces cracked. The whole table saw it, and *nobody* will put you on a quality hand this hand. They all know that you're trying to recover from broken aces. You're trying to get well. You're trying to overcome sadness.

Sad, sad you. A bad thing happened, and now you feel like you deserve a good thing as compensation. It doesn't work like that. You didn't make a mistake in the play of your aces. You just caught a bad break—which you compounded with bad play. *That* was the mistake. You have no one to blame but yourself.

Sad, sad you. Until you can deal with this sort of very minor league adversity, until you can get your aces cracked and come back strong and correct on the very next hand, then you're not playing Killer Poker. You're just playing around—and much more sadness lies ahead.

> *There is a play you can make when your aces get cracked, but it requires the right kind of cards. Since everyone saw your aces get cracked, they figure that you might now go on tilt. Should you happen to catch premium cards on your next hand, you can play them exactly as if you were on tilt, and make money on the looseness that your supposed bad beat inspires in your foes.*

Getting Your Mind Right

The point I wish to stress—and it simply cannot be stressed too much—is that your successful poker depends on your state of mind. To quote Strother Martin, the captain in *Cool Hand Luke,* "You've got to get your mind right." You need to reach the point where having your aces cracked affects you *no differently* from having your aces stand up. Why? For the reasons outlined above. If adversity cracks your state of mind along with your aces, then you open yourself up to a cascade of negative outcomes. At that point, the cracked aces become merely the nuclear trigger leading to the devastating plume of radioactive fallout to follow.

Lou Krieger, author of *Hold'em Excellence,* puts forth the concept of giving your opponents a narrow target to shoot at. According to Lou's logic, if you play very few hands, but play those hands strongly, you don't leave your foes much room for attack.

Well, suppose you've done that. Suppose you've played squeaky-tight poker all night long and created a circumstance where everyone knows that when *this guy* is in the pot, they can expect a strong hand played strongly. In order to preserve this image, you have been very careful not to get out ahead of your hands, thus putting yourself in the position of having to drive-bluff with inferior cards. In other words, you have earned respect—and a modicum of fear—from the other players.

Now here comes a hand (like those dad-ratted aces) that you play perfectly, but end up losing. Smarting from the loss, you limp in on the next hand—an uncharacteristically weak play from an uncharacteristically early position. The other players tune into this, for it's not like you to be in the pot on two hands in a row—especially just flat-calling. You seem to be losing your tightness.

One particularly attentive player decides to test you. He fires a raise at you from late position. You know from past experience with this guy that his raises don't necessarily correspond to his card values. You think about raising him back, but the loss on that last hand has rendered you temporarily timid. Now you're in trouble, because now you're out of position with a hand of secondary value against an opponent who has both the initiative and any possible hand. You fold on the flop or the turn, having surrendered several bets that you really didn't have to part with. Now you've had two bad outcomes on two consecutive hands. Overcome by the desire to get well, you play the next hand, play it badly, and dig yourself deeper into your hole. You do not, needless to say, have your mind right at this moment.

There are, among the many kinds of tilt, these two: hard tilt and soft tilt. Hard tilt you know very well. You see it happen every day, where a player takes a bad beat, feels deeply wronged by the universe, and starts raising with reckless abandon. Soft tilt is a little subtler. Inspired by the same sense of being wronged, you loosen up your starting requirements *just a little*. You back off on your aggressiveness *just a little*. Your performance thus drops off *just a little*. Each incremental degradation in the quality of your play merely paves the way for more of same. You go on tilt by degrees.

Hard tilt is easy to recognize. You see yourself going nuts on hand after hand and you say, "Whoa, wait a minute, this ain't right!" You pick yourself up and walk away from the game, taking time to recapture your cool. Having spotted the flash fire, you put it out before it burns out of control.

Soft tilt, however, is sneaky stuff. You can be deep into it before you even know you're there. Worse, it doesn't even take a bad beat to put you there. Sometimes a winning session and your own inflated sense of self can put you on soft tilt. If you've been running well and find yourself well ahead in the game, it's easy to justify opening up the valve a little, playing a few more hands, and speculating on a few more draws. After all, you're a superior player, right? The outcomes prove that, right?

Wrong! Positive outcomes don't demonstrate superior play. I'm going to repeat that and put it in a little box because it's so important.

> *Positive outcomes don't demonstrate superior play.*

Superior play may *lead* to positive outcomes, but you can also catch lucky. It's when you confuse catching lucky with playing well that the demons start to sneak in.

Get your mind right. Recognize that nothing matters in poker except making the correct decision on this hand and this bet, regardless of what came before or what may follow. If you do this one thing—concentrate on making the right decision—you may or may not be rewarded by positive outcomes, but you certainly won't be punished by soft tilt.

EXPECTATION

The Butterfly Effect is a phenomenon known to meteorologists and other students of—well, of phenomena like the

Butterfly Effect. What it says, simply, is that a butterfly batting its fragile wings in Burundi can, under the right atmo-
spheric conditions, trigger a typhoon in Japan. It's science's
way of saying that everything is connected and anything is
possible.

Just as that butterfly in Burundi affects the weather in
Tokyo, things that happen to you far away from the poker
table affect how you play and whether you win or lose. Case
in point: I was driving to a poker tournament in Los
Angeles on a fine and sunny Saturday afternoon. I allowed
myself plenty of time to make the drive and still catch the
first flop. No way could I possibly be late, unless I encountered some outrageous traffic, but why would there be outrageous traffic on a Saturday afternoon?

Hell, it's Los Angeles. Why wouldn't there be?

The freeway was a parking lot. So I got off the freeway—
bailed, in the vernacular. No problem. I knew a great bail to
the card club. Still no way I was going to be late—unless
there happened to be a big stuck truck blocking my bail.

To make a long, excruciating story less long and therefore less grim, I missed the first flop by two minutes. This
should not have been a problem, except that a dealer had
called in sick, so the alternate players' list was longer than
usual. So I didn't get into the tournament at all.

Big deal, you say? So I missed a tournament—so what?
Here's what: Having driven all that way, having weathered
traffic, stuck trucks, long stoplights, and stupid drivers, I
was in no mood to turn around and drive back home. Even
though I'd had every intention of playing in the tournament only, I soon found myself with a rack of chips and a
seat in a live game.

Not even the game I wanted! The game I wanted (the
game filled with known weakies and Wallies at a limit I felt
comfortable playing) was booked solid, with a long list of

eager waiters. So I settled instead for a game I *didn't* want, just because I felt I was *owed* somehow. Which phrase do you think most accurately describes my state of mind at the time: (a) cool, calm, and collected; or (b) steaming before I even sat down? I had had my expectation *defeated,* damn it, and the first available patron was by golly gonna *pay!* Guess who the first available patron turned out to be? That's right—me. I'd had the expectation of playing in a tournament, and the explosive defeat of that expectation put me on tilt.

We set out for the card room, club, or casino with the best of intentions: We're only going to play *our* game at *our* stakes. Then something small and unforeseen happens—that Butterfly Effect—and the option we want is no longer available. Maybe the game just broke. Maybe a dealer went home sick. Maybe the new shift boss thinks your favorite game is loony-tunes and won't spread it anymore. Maybe they're filming a stupid TV commercial outside the club and you get shut out of a tournament or a ring game in the time it takes you to detour around the key grip—whatever.

Anything can happen. If you don't expect it to happen, if you don't plan for it and prepare for it, it can put you on tilt. After that, well, you know. We crash, we burn, and we drive home with regret.

Which leads us to this observation:

> ***Discipline means more than folding bad hands.***

Discipline informs every part of a winning player's game. Its lack in any aspect of play can put the best player into a tailspin. Discipline starts—has to start—before we even sit down to play.

Think about this next time you're driving to your favorite poker spot. Somewhere ahead of you in the immediate future is *something you haven't planned for.* Maybe some chadhole will cut you out of a parking spot right by the front door—and flip you the bird when you claim you saw it first. Maybe some clumsy porter will spill hot coffee on you. Maybe some flipperbrain will chase you to the river with cheese, and get there with the world's lamest two-out draw. Something. It's bound to be something. Now the question is, Will you roll with the punches, using your flexibility, consciousness, and awareness to keep from making a bad situation worse? Or will you pull out the first available metaphorical firearm and, in your ill humor, shoot yourself in the foot?

Preparation helps. It helps to preview the possible disasters that can befall you in the poker realm. Remind yourself of the things that can go wrong, so that if they do go wrong, you won't put yourself on tilt.

- I could get a flat tire en route.
- The club could be closed.
- The lists could be infuriatingly long.
- The games could be terrible.
- The competition could be too tough.
- The dealer could be incompetent or rude.
- My foes could be obnoxious.
- The cards could betray me.
- My opponents' long shots could get there.
- My good hands could get cracked.
- My hand could be fouled.
- My drink could be spilled.
- My eggs could be runny.
- The joint could be robbed.

This merely scratches the surface of what could go wrong. I encourage you to think about it, *really* think about it. Prospect your own future. Investigate what lies ahead, or anyway what might lie ahead, for the sake of taking a strategic detour in time. Even down there on the level of the basic play of hands, it's useful to project the possibilities in advance.

Say you've been playing $20–$40 hold'em, and the player on your left hasn't raised once in the last three hours. This has given you a significant strategic advantage, one you have exploited by making more than your share of real estate raises and stealing more than your share of blinds. It's been so long since Lefty let one fly that you start to believe it's not even possible. Then he does, and it catches you flat-footed. Because you had stopped anticipating a raise from this player, you don't immediately know what to do. In your hasty thinking, you allow yourself to reach the wrong conclusion—*he's playing me*—instead of the obvious conclusion—*he finally woke up with a hand.* After you've peed away a bunch of bets, you wish you'd been better prepared.

Can you think of another example where your failure to anticipate a bad occurrence, or even just an unexpected one, had a negative effect on your play? Here's one of mine: I had called a raise pre-flop against one opponent with A-9 suited, and the flop came 9-x-x. I bet, and my single opponent raised. At that moment, a young hotshot not in the hand suddenly recognized me.

"I know you," he said. "You're that writer guy. Man, you suck!" Yes, he really said that. Hey, not everyone has manners. I was unprepared for his comment, and it rattled me—punched me right in my pride. I don't claim to be a world-class player, but I don't think I *suck.* In any event, I was momentarily knocked off balance. For a frenzied, out-of-control instant, I forgot where I was in the hand. I forgot that my opponent, a known trickster, was most likely trying to steal the pot with his raise. Instead, I found myself focused on how embarrassed I would be—I, *that writer guy*—if

I called all the way to the river and lost to an overpair or a set—especially if I had to show that I made a questionable call with my A-9 in the first place. Best to fold now, and hold humiliation at bay. So I folded. My opponent revealed his stone bluff, and the hotshot crowed, "I was right, you *do* suck!"

Look, I don't hold my mistakes against me. I've made them before, and lord knows I'll make them again. If I had it to do over again, I'd have alerted myself ahead of time to the dangers of other players' rudeness and my own pride-and-fear matrix. No matter—like they say at Chernobyl, that's fuel under the reactor now.

But if I don't learn from my mistakes, then I'm at the ongoing mercy of the Butterfly Effect. So I make every effort to take a note on the experience, and the next time I'm whacked upside the head by the explosive defeat of my expectations, I hope and trust that I'll be strong enough and disciplined enough to walk away unharmed.

How about you? Do you learn from your mistakes? Or does every little Tokyo typhoon take you by surprise? The worst ones start in Burundi, you know—and we never see them coming at all.

> *Unexpected outcomes affect everyone. Next time you see a player suffer any kind of unanticipated setback, recognize that he is, for the next few moments at least, vulnerable to attack.*

Why We Play

Why do you play poker? The rote answer, of course, is to *win money*. That's the rote answer, possibly even the best answer, but is it the *only* answer? Is it really?

Can you honestly say that the *only* reason you *ever* play

poker is to earn money? Even if that's your sole motivation, can you honestly say that you don't derive secondary benefit, psychic income, as it were, from playing the game well and dominating your opponents? Do you experience *no* special thrill when that third spade hits the board on the river, giving you the nut flush? Do you get *no* visceral kick out of raking in a huge pot and stacking all those chips? Do you experience no glow of pride when you're lugging three or four heavy racks to the cage, with all those admiring (and envious) eyes upon you as you pass?

Okay, then, you're the purest-motivated poker player who's ever drawn breath. There's just one problem: You're not human.

Let's face it, we get off on poker. We all do. You do. I do. Everyone who plays the game gets off on it to some degree. If they didn't, they wouldn't play. Why would they? There are so many other enjoyable and profitable things they could do with their time.

Look, I'm not trying to talk you out of playing poker, and I'm not trying to kill the joy you feel when you play. I'm just pointing out that, no matter how pure we think our motivation is, there are hidden rewards that draw us all to the game.

To prove this point to yourself, take a moment to make a *dividend list,* an account of all the big and little pleasures that poker gives you. Above and beyond the obvious reward of money won, how does poker float your boat?

- I get to be a bully.
- It's a mental workout; I find the challenge deeply satisfying.
- Poker makes the mundane problems of my life disappear for a while.
- It feeds my greed.

- I experience pleasure when the cards break my way.
- I get to feel superior to other people.
- I enjoy being tricky and deceptive.
- There's often interesting conversation.
- Food and drink are cheap or free.
- It kills time.
- No one from my "real life" can find me there.
- I experience camaraderie.
- I feel proud when I play well.
- I buy things I want with the money I win.
- I can be king of the hill.

Looking at my dividend list, I'm surprised by two discoveries. First, poker is important to me as a diversion and a time sink; second, I like to push people around, and poker offers an outlet for that urge. Looking at your dividend list, what discoveries do you make?

I once saw two small boys trying to walk on the top of a split-rail fence. It quickly became clear that they were engaged in a competition to see who could go farther, faster. I found myself wondering why boys as young as six or seven would be so caught up in competition. Perhaps, I mused, it's genetically encoded, a survival characteristic. Competition, after all, keeps us striving, growing and moving forward as individuals and as a species. Without it, we'd still be living in trees wondering where our next banana was coming from.

So then it may be that the kick we get out of playing poker is simply the kick of winning. When we win, when we're rakin' and rackin' that big pile of chips, endorphins flood our brains. We receive an immediate and direct chemical reward for having *won the game*. That, ladies and gentlemen, is the buzz of poker—the buzz we chase, whether we admit it or not. That's what brings us back for more. So let's not kid ourselves that it's only about the money.

Now, what if it were otherwise? What if it weren't about the thrill of victory, but the thrill of defeat instead?

Some sad sacks seem to have gotten their cranial wires crossed, so that they receive a direct chemical reward not for winning but for losing. These people are punishing themselves because they feel that they don't deserve to win. We know these people as compulsive gamblers or even compulsive losers. They seem to take pleasure in peeing their money away. They can't help it; some people just love to lose. We can thus parse the poker world into two types: those who see themselves as winners and take pleasure in winning; and those who see themselves as losers and take pleasure in losing.

This raises a delicate subject. If it's true that the poker world is filled with compulsive losers, what moral responsibility do the rest of us have? Should we save them from themselves by not taking their money? Should we tell them to quit playing, even though their gain is our loss? Should we encourage them to gamble even more, knowing that their twisted pleasure is our profit? Should we try to teach them to play better so they don't hurt themselves so badly? Or should we go on bleeding them dry, rationalizing that, "If I didn't do it, someone else would"?

I can't resolve this debate, and it's not my place to try. All I can say is this: If winning at poker rewards you in your soul, then you're fine, but if losing at poker rewards you in your soul, then you'd better change to checkers.

5

♣♠♦♥

BEING AND BECOMING

♣♤◇♡

ASCENDANCE

People play poker for money. It's more than a way of keeping score. It's the thing that gives the game meaning. As
you know from your own experience, if you don't play for
money, you don't take the game seriously, and you don't
make good decisions because, *hell, who cares?* So we play
for money to ensure that our decisions have consequences.
That's what makes poker worthwhile; that's what makes
poker *poker.*

After a while, you build up a tolerance to money.
Around the kitchen table of your youth, you could lose 65
cents in a game of anaconda and feel like the world had
come to an end. Now you can endure swings of hundreds
of dollars or more without batting an eye. You've become
more comfortable, over time, with playing for higher
stakes.

The problem is, if you become too comfortable, you stop
caring once again. Stakes that once made your heart race
become, over time, so low that you can't win or lose an
amount that's meaningful to you. There's no real incentive
for playing well. This is why high stakes players who come

slumming in low-limit games often play so poorly. The money doesn't matter, so they don't bother to bring their "A" game. Even if you're a $6–$12 player and find yourself in a $2–$4 game while waiting for a seat in $6–$12, you may not be playing your best. This is, of course, ridiculous. Killer Poker means always bringing your "A" game. Remember the prime directive: *Go big or go home.*

The trick, then, is finding the right money level for your comfort. You want the money to matter enough to focus your attention—but then again not to matter so much that you end up playing scared. Why? Because if you're scared, you play differently. Outside your comfort zone, things quickly fall apart.

Example: You've been kicking it at the $4–$8 level, and you decide to take a shot at (oh, let's be outrageously brave here) $20–$40. Maybe you've never played $20–$40 before; maybe you have. In any case, you don't play this game regularly, and it does not escape your attention that a single hand at this limit can net—or cost—you more than an entire session at $4–$8. You tell yourself not to be scared. Maybe you aren't even scared—but you're a little uncomfortable. Admit it, you are.

No problem, you tell yourself: Just screw down your starting requirements, pay attention, play quality cards, *concentrate,* and you'll do just fine.

Then this hand comes up: You're in late position with A-Q suited. It's folded around to you, and you figure this is a perfect opportunity to assault the blinds, so you plunk down a raise. The button and the small blind fold. Perfect! You wouldn't mind stealing the blinds here. It would do wonders for your comfort. Alas, the big blind calls. He eyes you curiously as he does so. Does he recognize you as a newbie? Does he know that you're outside your comfort zone? Maybe. Maybe not. He *does* know this for sure: You're not a regular, because *he's* a regular, and he's never seen you before.

Unfortunately for you, he has a *program bet* (a predetermined betting sequence or strategy) that he uses on players he's never seen before. What he does is, he check-calls any flop, then check-raises any turn. He can do this because he's *comfortable* at this limit, and if the gambit doesn't work, he won't miss the chips—especially when he considers how much information about (and dominance over) you he stands to collect. So this is what he does to you, and unless you flop a monster, his program bet will put you in a bad place. If you fold now, you look weak, passive, and exploitable. If you raise back, or even call, you're committing *a lot more money* than you're used to committing on any single bet. Trapped thus between Scylla and Charybdis, you throw your hand away. Better that than your money, right?

Just to cheese you off (for this is part of his program-bet strategy) your opponent shows you the rags with which he bluffed you out. Now you feel hot, embarrassed, and ridiculous. Where does your session go from here? Into free fall, and thence, if you're not careful, into the toilet.

The next hand you pick up is A-K suited, but you're afraid to raise with it, afraid to leave yourself open to the same sort of attack you just endured. So you flat-call instead, hoping to flop big and become the trapper instead of the trappee. The flop comes 9-x-x, and your now-nemesis bets right out. Does he have a nine? He easily could, given that you didn't raise him off any moderate small blind holding pre-flop. You've got overcards, so you call. You call again on the turn. By the time the river comes down, you're looking at a ragged board with no ace and no king, and your only hope of winning the hand is if your opponent is on a stone bluff. He checks, inducing you to bet, which you do because you're damned if you're gonna show fear. He

calls, delighted to take his top pair, good kicker against anything you have. He wins, you lose. That's not bad luck.
That's bad play. That's letting your own discomfort dictate
your choices. Next thing you know, you're picking up your
chips (before you lose them all) and heading back down to
the $4–$8 game, hoping to recoup your losses, confidence,
and dignity.

Where did you go wrong? You may have counted your
six outs—three aces and three kings—and determined that
the odds (pot odds, implied odds, tooth fairy odds—
whatever odds you were using) warranted your calls. But
this isn't about odds. It never was about odds. You yielded
so much initiative that it almost doesn't matter whether
you hit your hand or not. You were back on your heels, and
as we've already determined, *you can't strike from back on
your heels.*

> *Poker rewards initiative. The higher you play,
> the truer this becomes.*

So what's the solution? Never move up? Stay at your
same comfort level forever? That hardly seems satisfactory.
Okay, so here are some things you can do to make that
jump to the next comfort level less hazardous to your financial and emotional health.

1. Study the game. Before you put big money into a
    (relative to you) big bet game, take some time to
    watch—*really watch*—the action at the table. Fa-
    miliarize yourself with the players and their tactics
    (and their program bets). I'm not talking about a
    few hands, either; I'm talking *hours* of watching
    instead of playing, so that when it's your turn to
    take a seat in the game, you don't feel like a total
    fish out of water (or even just a total fish).

2. Refine your knowledge. Go back to your poker texts and read up on mid-limit to high-limit play. They *do* play differently up there, and the moves you use at $4–$8 and $6–$12 just won't cut it at $20–$40 and above. Low-limit play, in general, is about playing the cards. Up there in the stratosphere (or even the troposphere) it's more about playing the players than the cards. Until you're ready to embrace this distinction, you're not ready to move up.

3. Fortify your bankroll. Make sure you have enough money so that you don't have to play scared. You absolutely will not succeed at higher limits until they don't seem like higher limits to you, because scared money will skew your decisions every time. You'll check when you should bet and call when you should raise; your own passivity will cripple you. So come well armed or don't come at all.

It's worth working on your game and your mind-set to the point where you can move up. Both the riches and the richness of poker await you there. If you're nervous, just remember: Once you learn to swim, it doesn't matter how deep the water gets.

> *Before you move up to a higher limit, ask a player in that game what the game is like. He'll be flattered that you asked—and give you a wealth of information you can use to prepare yourself for the plunge.*

Comparisons

Have you ever watched an opponent play and said to yourself, "That's how you do it; that's how I want to play."

Some people find it difficult to admire another player's play. Their egos won't let them. They fear, in some reptilian sense, that if they acknowledge the superior play of an opponent they somehow lose status themselves. This is, in a word, bosh. John Fortescue said it best (back in 1471!) "Comparisons are odious." Each of us is precisely as good as we are. No better, no worse. We're all trying to close the gap between the ability we have and the ability we want. The skill level or expertise of our foes doesn't matter at all, except as a function of whether we choose to play against them and what we can learn from them.

On this subject, *do you have a mentor?* Is there someone in your poker life who knows more about poker than you do, and is willing to share this knowledge? I'm not talking about hiring a teacher (though many people do that). I'm talking about honoring a superior player by *just being interested* in what he has to say. For the cost of probably no more than a meal, you can get a world of insight and strategy from a more experienced and able player. I still remember three valuable things I learned from my mentor in our first conversation.

1. *Bet the river.* Make the other guy make the tough decision.
2. *Go with your gut.* More often than not, your opponent has the hand you think he has.
3. *Be a mensch.* It's better for the game and better for your bankroll too.

Could I have derived this information on my own? Yes—eventually. Why wait for eventually, when so much good information is already out there? If you don't want a mentor, you can always lurk on Internet discussion groups like rec.gambling.poker and just read and learn while the opinions and the wisdom fly. If you find that you don't really want a mentor, take a moment to ask yourself why. Do you believe you have nothing else to learn? Or can it be that you can't face the low status that being "a student" seems to imply?

Recall your Fortescue. Comparisons are odious! And counterproductive too.

Yet how we burden ourselves with envy or resentment when we see a major player running over the table—*our* table—and we find ourselves saying, "Why him? Why not me?" In the dark glower of our rationalizing mind a voice answers, "He's no better than me. He's just lucky." Of course, that's not it at all.

A player in the late stages of a tournament puts a terrific read on an opponent and calls down a huge bet with a hand that's ever so thinly better than his foe's. Is that just luck? If not luck, then what is it? Skill? Intuition? Courage? What does he have that you and I don't?

Hey, maybe he's just gifted. Maybe he's a virtuoso with a knack for making magic at the poker table. Or maybe he's just well prepared. I'll bet if you ask him, he'd say something like, "Well, I work on my game all the time. I study my opponents every second that I'm at the table. I chart their tendencies. I know that the time will come when I'll face them in a critical situation and I want all the information I can get when that critical moment comes. The information is there. I just have to go get it."

So here is a player who has identified himself as a diligent *information gatherer*. That's not a virtuoso's gift; that's just lunch-bucket stuff. Anyone can do that—if they're willing to learn.

Look, I'm not saying that anyone who plays poker can become a top pro—any more than anyone who picks up a violin can become Jascha Heifetz. Some people *are* just naturally gifted, and we have to credit them for their gifts.

BEING AND BECOMING   149

At the same time, whether we have such gifts or not, we do have *our game,* and we do have the potential to take that game to its highest level.

We might call this *The Wade Boggs Paradigm.* Perennial baseball all-star Wade Boggs was a naturally gifted hitter with a lifetime batting average of .328. Yet every day of his career he went out there and took batting practice with a dedication bordering on obsession. Hey, if a naturally gifted practitioner like Wade Boggs found it appropriate to work on his game every day, don't you think the same applies to pluggers like us?

Of course, it does! Yet, there are strong disincentives. It's hard work to work on your game. You have to read books, run simulations, and think about things. Harder still is the need to confront yourself candidly and admit that "Not only am I not as good as the players I admire, I'm not even as good as I can be." In the face of that sad revelation, it's easy to say, "Oh well, I guess I'll just plug along and hope to catch lucky."

Don't fall into that trap. You don't have to. Sure, you may never win the World Series of Poker. You may never even be as good as that local pro who always seems to quit winners, but you can always be better than you are. You can always strive to improve your game. There will always be a gap between the player you are and the player you desire to be. Your job is not to eradicate the gap—you can't—but every day you can narrow it. No one, not even the top pros, can make any more progress than that.

WORSIFY

Sometimes your opponents just aren't bad enough. Sometimes you look around the table and see a bunch of good, solid players making good, solid plays. Your first recourse is to change games, and that's the option you should exercise if you can—get out from under superior foes. You may be afraid of the blow to your pride—but it's much better to lose face than to lose money, is it not?

Sometimes, though, circumstances conspire to cut off that line of retreat. Maybe the lists for other games are prohibitively long. Maybe there *are* no other games. We could argue that not playing at all is preferable to playing against superior foes, but hey, you're only human, right? Sometimes you just don't want to quit; nor, however, do you want to continue against superior foes. What to do?

You could try to play better. That seems reasonable. You could keep a low profile and wait with perfect patience for perfect situations. However, while it's true that keeping your head low in a foxhole will keep you from getting shot, it also won't let you advance. If you play that tight—the screws turned all the way clockwise—your good opponents will have an easy read on you and soon come to control you.

Then again, it may be that you're already playing about as well as you can play. Further, it may be that significantly improving your own play won't significantly enhance your chances of beating this particular field. So we come to a third alternative: *Make your opponents play worse!*

Put 'em on tilt, right? In a perfect world, you'd have the style and the strategies to put any group of foes on tilt. However, here we've postulated superior foes, and they're not just going to roll over for you. So let's say that you *can't* put these guys on tilt, not total nose- and wallet-open tilt. The best you can do is to incrementally degrade the quality of their play—worsify them. Here are some ways to do that.

Blow Smoke

God no, I'm not talking about blowing cigarette smoke in your foes' faces. That would be just rude, and while rudeness will certainly worsify some foes, I cannot, in the spirit of moral—not to say political—correctness, recommend that action. No, the kind of smoke I speak of blowing is the steady stream of friendly distraction, which while friendly as hell, is distracting as hell as well. Compliment people on their looks. Ask where they're from, what they do for a living. Ask why they played a certain hand a certain way. Do what you can to make thoughtful players think about something other than their play. You may look like a goofball. That's okay; if they think you're a goofball, it will make them underestimate your strength.

A simple math applies: It costs you a minute of concentration to tell that joke you know about the farmer's daughter and the traveling penguin, but it costs each of the other players a minute of their concentration to listen to the joke. Your expenditure of concentration is repaid multifold. The more brainpower you can get *anyone* to spend in contemplation of your joke, question, or inane observation, the less brainpower they have to spend on the correct analysis of your check-raise bluff.

Fuss

Squirm, and fidget. Yell at the football game on the big screen TV. Make fake angry phone calls on your cell phone. Complain about the food or the service or the weather or whatever. Create an air of tension around yourself. If you seem to be on the verge of *just losing control*, sensitive players will respond. Maybe they'll respond by becoming somewhat tenser themselves. Maybe they'll respond by incorrectly playing into you in anticipation of what they perceive to be your impending psychological meltdown. Either way, they're responding to image, not reality.

Even if they're smart enough to think, "Well, that's image, not reality," they're *still responding*. They're thinking about you and not about their game. That's a step in the right direction for you.

Have Fun

This is more or less the opposite of fussing, and when you abruptly change gears from fussing to having fun, it can have a very unsettling effect on your foes. Plus, if you manifest a merry mood, good players may wonder what's wrong with them—Why hasn't their superior play rendered you scared, sullen, and morose? *Don't you know how outclassed you are?* At the very least, having fun will keep you in a temperate state of mind until either your efforts to worsify the game, or the game's own momentum, cause some others to play poorly and your prospects in the game to improve. Oh heck, let's make it simple: Having fun is *never* a bad idea.

Many top players think that they're immune to this class of nonsense. If you act friendly, act badly, act nuts, act out, or "act" in any sense, many top players will look at you with indulgent amusement. They find themselves thinking, "He doesn't really expect me to fall for that, does he? How can he imagine that that nonsense is going to put me off my game?" Again, if they're thinking about you in any sense, even through the filter of indulgent amusement, you've already won. They think your nonsense doesn't affect them, but they're wrong. You're inside their head, and worsification has begun.

Does it work? Of course, it works! You might have a very good foe who insists that he ignores all forms of noise, table talk, and image play and makes his decisions based strictly on cards, chips, tells, and position, but even if he *knows* that you're horsing around, he's still playing into your image. He's thinking about you when he should be thinking about himself. If he's wrong—if he thinks you're clueless when you're not—then he'll start to make mistakes.

Suppose you push a hand that doesn't really deserve to be pushed, like A-8. You catch a flop of A-8-x and drive that hand all the way to the river, where, alas, your opponent catches a king to make his A-K stand up. Bad luck, right? Wrong. Opportunity! Because now you *can't stop talking* about the stupid beat you just took—a beat that your savvy foes know wasn't really a beat at all because you started with an inferior hand. You create the impression of someone who is a *great fool.*

When you next get involved with a hand—this time with big tickets—you get action you wouldn't have gotten if you'd just stayed quiet and minded your own business. Then when you turn over a legitimate hand, your foes don't know whether you're inconsistent, clueless, or messing with their minds. A combination of one lucky flop, one unlucky river, and your aggressive projection of image has improved your situation considerably. You've lost a pot and won a pot, but more important, you've worsified your foes.

Image Play

This entire class of behavior—image play—is a crucial part of many people's play. They rely more on image than they do on math skills, memory, courage, or luck. You may have used image as a tool many times in the past. Think now about what images you have portrayed and what steps you took to make sure that your opponents got the message you were trying to send. I suspect that you weren't always as bold in your image plays as you might have been, because pride, embarrassment, or a sense of propriety held you back. If that's so, remember that embarrassment is a small enough price to pay in pursuit of profit. It costs you nothing—*nothing*—to project a wild, crazy, angry, or a jovial image, or even an unutterably stupid one. If it earns you so much as a single bet from a single opponent, it has made itself worthwhile.

Look, a tough game is a tough place to be. Against really good competition, the best you can hope for is to hold your own. This is not the point, of course—you want to hold *theirs!* So your first move should always be to try to find a better game. If you can't do that, then do everything in your power to degrade the quality of your opponents' play. The more you worsify them, the more you "betterfy" your odds.

> *You won't know which images work well for you until you have experimented with many. Some images work well in one game but not in another. Further, image is often wasted on players who aren't paying attention. If you aren't paying attention to—and cultivating—your image(s), you're overlooking a profitable part of your game.*

Protecting Your Blinds

One thing you always see in a tough hold'em game is incessant theft of blinds, and all your attempts to worsify your foes will not change the fact that they're gonna come after you. Obviously you need to account for this and plan for this if you want to or have to play in tough games, so let's take a look at habitual blind stealers and see how we can deal with the steal.

Habitual blind stealers assume that your random hand plus their positional advantage give them a consistent advantage, and a consistent opportunity to push you around.

And they're right. They do have an edge in this circumstance. So we need to develop countermeasures to put inveterate blind-thieves in their place. Here's one I call "Around Town."

First divide your possible starting hands into three categories: downtown, midtown, and uptown. Downtown hands are crummy cards—little poison, jackthree, and so on. Midtown cards are semiplayable hands like middle pairs and certain suited connectors. Uptown cards are premium holdings: big tickets and big pairs. After you have identified a certain foe as someone capable of the pure steal, you then make your response according to your holding: surrender downtown, reraise uptown, and flat-call midtown.

Downtown: If you have just purely dreadful cards, you're just giving away your money when you call. You know he's on a steal, but since your hand truly sucks, his two random cards are likely to be better than (certainly can't be worse than) the two random cards you hold. You also know that blind-stealers are not likely to be frightened by reraises from the big blind. You can be pretty sure that he'll call your raise, since he has both position and long experience on his side. So if you bluff-raise in this circumstance, you're launching a bluff you'll have a lot of difficulty driving through.

Surrender this blind, and wait for one that you can play more effectively against him. Notice that surrendering this blind actually encourages him to try the move again, when the circumstances might be much more favorable to you.

Midtown: If you have middling cards, play a modified version of hit-to-win. Since his steal-raise means he's on anything-or-nothing, any flop that even partly hits your hand figures to put you ahead. With cards of medium strength, you're no worse than equal to any random hand,

and you're getting pot odds to call: 3.5-1 if everyone, including the small blind, has folded in front of you.

If the flop is scary (coordinated high cards), you can release your hand in the face of significant heat. Again, to come out betting is problematic because he won't credit you with big cards (or otherwise, where was your reraise pre-flop?). If the flop hits your hand or seems not to hit his, you can check-call the flop and check-raise the turn, intending either to drive him off the hand or be able to show down a little something. Frequently against a blind-thief, even a little something is more than enough against the total nothing that he was too proud or stubborn to fold when you raised.

Note that when you check-call the flop and check-raise the turn, you're representing a *successful trap play*. Even if your opponent credits you with a bluff in this situation, the fact that *he started on a total bluff* makes it difficult for him to call. Much more difficult than, say, calling your pre-flop reraise from the big blind. Pre-flop, he figures you're just trying to play back at him. On the turn, when the hand is well defined, he has to give credit to the idea that your random cards have connected to something on the board. Plus, you strung him along, looking for a chance to trap. All of this adds up to the possibility that he'll fold his hand right here, and the further possibility that he'll squirrel around with your blinds a little less in the future.

Uptown: If you have big cards, you'll simply reraise pre-flop and bet any flop that could conceivably have hit a hand worth a pre-flop reraise from the blind. For instance, you might reraise with A-Q, then bet when a naked king hits the board. Your opponent's steal-raise tells you that he's on a random hand, but your reraise tells him that you're *not* on a random hand. Your reraise, then, gives you control not just of any flop that contains court cards or ace, but really of any flop at all. Don't slow down unless you encounter resistance. You want not just to win the pot but also to send the message through aggressive countermeasures to leave your blind alone!

These are the basic guidelines for Around Town. You can, of course, vary your play. For instance, if you've had to surrender several blinds in a row, go ahead and reraise the next time to make your opponent think you've finally caught a blind hand worth aggressively defending. Conversely, if you know that your foe will bet any flop when he has you one-on-one, then flat-call your monster hands and see what real trap opportunities the flop or the turn may bring.

By playing a predefined strategy such as Around Town, you do three useful things. First, you give yourself the benefit of preplanning. Second, you give yourself new confidence in playing your blinds, turning what was previously an area of vulnerability and weakness into an area of opportunity and strength. Third, and most important, you get into the habit of thinking ahead. This is a habit that pays dividends in all facets of your game, not just in the play of blinds.

When you stop playing *hands* and *cards,* and start playing *situations,* your game takes a quantum leap forward.

SITUATIONS

Good cards come and go, but profitable situations happen all the time. There's always something going on at the table, something you can respond to if you're smart enough and bold enough to play the situation, regardless of the cards you hold.

Say you're playing mid-limit hold'em against a solid lineup. These are good players, and you know that you're not going to beat them with cards alone. You have to out-play them too. You need to exploit situations. So you start to look for them. (While, at the same time, *always* staying on the lookout for a better game, because a table full of weak players is the best situation of all.)

You notice, for example, that one of your foes loves little pairs and pushes them aggressively before the flop. If your read on your opponent is solid, here's a situation where you can call with nothing at all, then simply bet into any scary flop and win the pot right there. Does it matter what your cards are? No! You've recognized a situation—your opponent pushes little pairs too far—and exploited it accordingly. Perhaps you've even refined the situation by folding on an earlier, less scary flop and thus trained your opponent to take your situation-based bet at face value.

Some situations are no-brainers: You know what you're going to do with A-A in late position—raise; and you know what you're going to do with 7-2 offsuit early—fold. What will you do with that T-9 suited in middle position? If the pot is opened in front of you, you're gone, but if no one else has yet jumped in, suddenly you have a situation—one you can turn to your advantage.

You might take that T-9 and raise with it, representing a big pair. If the flop comes very big or very little, you can bet out and maybe win right there. If the flop comes middle—smacks you squarely in the heart of your holding—then you can proceed in all sorts of creative and profitable ways. Why? Because you set up the situation by raising before the flop with an unlikely hand.

First you create the situation, then you exploit it. Is this risky? Sure it's risky. Smart players may get wise to your tactics. After all, they're playing situations too, and they're always on the lookout for mooks who step out of line. Then again, some players never look up from their hands. They wouldn't know a situation if it bit them on the butt. They're playing kosher poker, and they may even be doing well with it—*but not as well as they could.* For example, they never attack a blind that's there for the taking unless they absolutely have the cards to back it up. To me, that's a squandered opportunity. If I think the blinds will fold, I'll raise with anything. What's the worst that can happen? I might lose a bet or two. What's the *best* that can happen? I might take control of the game.

When you start thinking about poker in terms of situations and not just cards, you realize that the entire session—in fact your entire poker career—is just one big situation that you will ultimately exploit either well, poorly, or not at all. Those who make the most of the "big situation" are the ones who strive to take over any table they play at, and to dominate it according to their skills and abilities.

You know what I'm talking about. You've seen it happen countless times. You're sitting in some quiet little poker game filled with rocks and Cally Wallies when suddenly—boom!—a new player sits down and immediately starts betting and raising out of all proportion to everyone else's style and desire.

He has encountered a situation, a weak, tight table, and turned it into a different situation, a weak tight table dominated by one strong player. Whose chances do you like best in that situation?

Here's another situation, one common to Omaha/8: You see the flop along with two other players, and it comes K-9-3. They check in front of you, and you check too; nobody has nuttin'. The turn brings an offsuit five. Your foes check and you bet. One drops, and one calls. You put him on a low draw or a low straight draw or both, because you've already identified him as someone who will call-

and-chase, call-and-chase. If a third low card comes, you can surrender the pot, but if the river card is big and scary, you can bet with impunity and win the pot when he folds.

What if he's tricky? What if he check-raises the river? That won't happen. You've already identified him as not tricky, haven't you? If you thought he was tricky you wouldn't make this play in the first place.

Notice that in this example I didn't even bother speculating on what cards you held. Your cards don't matter. All that matters is the way you discover, analyze, and exploit the situation.

> *Next time you start your session, identify which players are "true value" players and which ones are frisky like you. Define strategies for situations against each type.*

Situation and Nonsituation Players

We can, then, divide the poker universe into those players who play situations and those who do not—S-type and N-type players, if you will. S-type players are not concerned with whether a given bet is rewarded or relinquished. Though they would prefer to win, S-type players are prepared to accept any outcome, and they incorporate that outcome into their overall strategy for the game. N-type players, on the other hand, sweat every bet, rue every loss, and seek to get well as quickly as possible. Contrast S-type and N-type responses to the following situation:

An S-type player, holding an ace with a medium kicker in late position bets into a flop of A-A-K. He gets called by one opponent, who also calls the turn. At this point our S-type hero puts his opponent on a straight draw, knowing that while *he* wouldn't play that draw, many of his foes are not nearly so sensible. A ten comes on the river. His opponent checks, hoping to check-raise, but the S-type player figures now that the only hand that can call him can beat him, so he just checks, then quietly mucks his big hand when his opponent shows the inevitable Q-J offsuit. He doesn't lament and he doesn't complain. He merely files away this information for future reference: "My worthy adversary here will take bad draws with bad odds. I'll try to give him that opportunity again real soon."

An N-type player in the same situation doesn't stop to consider what his opponent might be holding. All he knows is, "I've got trip aces; I'm one pair-card away from a monster full house!" He bets the flop and the turn exactly the way the S-type player did, but when that ten comes on the river, he doesn't pause to consider that he might be beaten, and he falls right into his opponent's check-raise snare. Not only that, when his foe shows down the winner, the N-type player angrily mucks his ace face-up and vows (either silently or aloud) to wreak revenge on the thin-drawing moron who sucked out on him. He doesn't realize—he never will realize—that his opponent has handed him a massive opportunity for later conquest. He's too far lost in his pain to take future opportunities into account.

Forgetting for a moment that the N-type player's mishandling of the river cost him two big bets (about twice as much as the S-type player lost on the same hand), look at what the hand has done to the N-type player's self-control, sense of well-being, and image. From this point forward, he's bent on revenge. His game, such as it was, has just gone out the window. All the savvy S-type players around him have watched this embarrassment take place and are now busy planning strategies to exploit his growing weakness.

When S-type players confront one another, they parry and feint, hoping to eke out a marginal advantage. When

N-type players confront one another, their mutual lack of skill makes their match-up a coin toss. When N-type players confront S-type players, however, the N-type players never stand a chance. An N-type player can only hope to beat an S-type player in the limited circumstance of running very lucky and then quickly running away.

So you have to ask yourself what kind of player you want to be. If you're going up against tough, knowledgeable opponents, you have to be tough and knowledgeable too. You can't just wait to get good cards and hope they stand up. Your strongest opponents will pummel you through good cards and bad cards alike, so that by the time you actually do catch some cards, you'll be so weakened from the attack that you won't be able to make the most of your temporary edge.

Money flows from the weak to the strong. You have to decide for yourself on which side of that transaction you want to be.

CONSISTENCY

To prove that my high school years were more than a teenage wasteland of nickel-ante poker games and futile assaults on the virtues of various young ladies, I now quote Ralph Waldo Emerson, who I studied extensively (or so I am told) in literature class, and who had this (or so I am told) to say:

> *"A foolish consistency is the hobgoblin of little minds . . ."*

How, you might ask, does this amorphous aphorism, foisted upon me in lit class, apply to poker? Here's how: To win at poker, you have to play consistently good poker. This we know. All the pundits agree: Come with your "A" game or don't come at all. Ah-ha, yes, but also to win at poker you must occasionally play deceptive poker, which means inconsistent poker, which means not consistently good poker. We have a paradox here, and I heighten its importance by setting it off in a paradox box:

> *For the sake of deception, you must sometimes play wrong on purpose.*

Suppose you're playing *hold'em* and you pick up 7-6 suited. It's a trash hand, right? You know it's trash, I know it's trash, even the mooks you play against know it's trash. The clear decision here is to fold. That's exactly the choice that "quality poker" mandates. There's no rationale for calling with this hand—but is there a rationale for raising?

Frequently a raise here will cost you both your pre-flop bets, because even if no one reraises you before the flop, you'll miss most flops and mostly have to throw that trash hand away. Then again, on those rare times when you do connect to this holding, none of the foolishly consistent hobgoblins you play against will put you on the hand you have. Plus, when you show down that ragamuffin hand, you'll really confound the small minds, so that when you next raise with A-A, it'll come out looking like 7-6 to them.

Raising situationally with hands that must hit the flop in order to work is not nearly so reckless a move as it appears—not if you're disciplined enough to get away from the hand if it misses, perceptive enough to know that it has hit but not sufficiently, and aggressive enough to drive it home completely when it's good. Of course, you don't want to make this play against wily opponents, but who wants to play against wily opponents anyway? Save this play for those times when your foes are consistent and weak.

Yes, I know that this flies in the face of the whole *little poison* thinking, but remember, we're talking about *raising*, not *calling*, which puts the strength of the hand in the *bet*, not the *cards*. Though I'd almost always fold this hand (and virtually never call with it) I will occasionally raise with it, when the situation is exactly right. I do it in the name of inconsistency.

Fortunately for us, weakness and consistency go hand in hand in many of our foes. For instance, weak opponents consistently raise with only premium hands. This makes them terribly easy to read, and there's no reason on the planet for a Killer Poker player ever to get trapped in a tangle against them. In another instance, weak opponents frequently make decisions based not on what they *think* you have, but on what they *hope* you have. It is to stimulate this wishful misthinking that we get into the whole sordid business of consistent inconsistency, and strongly played weak cards, in the first place.

Suppose your foe has Q-T offsuit, and you raise into him. If you raised consistently with only good cards, he'd know to put you on a quality hand, A-K or a big pair. He probably should fold, and possibly even knows it, but he doesn't want to fold. He wants to play; that's why he's here. That's why you flavor your play with a little inconsistency. You want to give this weak player a reason to believe that you have the hand he *wishes* you had instead of the hand you actually *do* have. Thus he calls when he shouldn't, and thus you crush him with his own delusive thinking.

So, yes, you're throwing off chips when you raise incorrectly, but at the same time you're encouraging your opponents to call incorrectly. Since there's many of them and only one of you, you end up making money on the margin. Remember also that bad raises are the seasoning in your play, not your steady diet. Most of the time you should be banging away at the pot with quality cards. That's most of the time—not all the time. And when you get out of line, do it with a raise, not a call.

Bad raises work because they help your image and sometimes allow you to win a pot you otherwise wouldn't get near. They create bluff opportunities and steal opportunities, and give you stronger control over the game as a whole. Bad *calls* do none of these. You endure all the downside of playing trash hands but reap none of the image rewards that come from pressing bad hands.

What we're talking about, really, is the difference between a microview and a macroview of poker.

> *In the microview, a hand is either profitable or not, playable or not. In the macroview, the hand only exists in the context of the game as a whole.*

In the macroview, profit comes not from winning individual pots but from taking over the table. Macroview poker doesn't excuse bad calls—nothing does that—but it does suggest a way to make bad raises for good reasons. You can allow yourself a temporary reversal of fortune—even the loss of a few promiscuous bets—if it serves your long-term goal of dominating and crushing your foes.

> *Here's an exercise that many players find tough:*
> **Get out of line!** *Make a bad raise at a bad time from a bad position and see what kind of dividends it yields. If nothing else, you will come to see yourself as someone capable of making unexpected moves, and that, in the macro sense, is very good for your game.*

Fantasy Poker

Do you fantasize about poker? When you're driving down the highway, sitting in boring meetings, or listening with half an ear to the kids telling you about their day at school,

do you find yourself thinking about check-raising an obvious bluffer and gleefully driving him off his hand? Do you
devour poker books, Internet chat, and the poker press like
it's poker porn? Does the contemplation of poker turn you
on? That's fine. I applaud that.

If you're going to fantasize, though, don't just fantasize,
fantasize constructively. When you think about your poker,
don't think about how good it would feel to win this hand
or that pot. Rather, when you think about poker—
departing from the point of pure pleasure—seek to con-
struct situations that amount to puzzles. "Given these
circumstances," tell yourself, "against these opponents, in
this type of game, how would I play this hand?" Then challenge yourself to come up with an elegant solution. It's a
lot like playing mental chess, and it looks a little like this:

> Okay, JV, you're in middle position in a $15–$30 *hold'em*
> game. The player on your right has been drinking Tequila
> Braindeaths and mouthing loudly about his bad luck for
> the last half hour. He's down to his last $100 and he seems
> very much in the mood to rack off and go home. How can
> you help him do it?
>
> *Well, let's see,* he has 20 redbirds left, which means he can
> get to the river one more time in a hand that's not raised
> on any street. If you raise and he calls pre-flop, then he's
> got six chips in already. Three more on the flop, and six
> on the turn means he'll be all-in with five chips on the
> river. Given his pouty and pixilated state of mind, you can
> pretty much count on him going pot-commit with any
> hand that calls a raise pre-flop.
>
> Also, given his pouty and pixilated state of mind, he'll
> probably call with an inferior hand. So you definitely want
> to go after him.
>
> Can't wait too long, either, because there are other sharks
> swimming in these waters, any one of whom will be happy
> to relieve ol' Drunky-tilty here of his last Big Ben. So you

need to be prepared to raise the very next hand that Drunky-tilty plays. You have the advantage of position— you get to act first after he makes the fatal decision to enter what (you hope) will be his last pot of the night.

So just calling is out of the question. You have to raise no matter what, and hope to get him one-on-one. Trouble is, your opponents know that. They won't put you on a big hand when you raise, and they're likely to reraise just to put the screws to you and take ol' Drunky-tilty's case money for themselves.

This means that *their* hand values will be correspondingly degraded; they could be in there with anything. So: Raise with any hand that's halfway playable. Anticipate a reraise, and if Drunky-tilty calls, plan on capping the betting no matter what you hold, to send a message to the reraiser that you do, in fact, have a real hand.

It's a two-pronged attack. You want to beat the reraiser with the power of your bets and then beat Drunky-tilty on the draw. So you bet any flop and bet any turn. By which time, if all has gone according to plan, the pre-flop reraiser has folded and Drunky-tilty is all-in with a hand he probably wouldn't have played at all if he'd had his wits about him—which he doesn't. That is what gives you your edge and it's why you went after him in the first place. If all goes according to plan, you'll rake the pot and send Drunky-tilty home to bed.

Don't get greedy! If Drunky-tilty calls (or raises) pre-flop, and you totally miss the flop, don't feel obliged to follow through. Since you have already predicted that he's pot-committed, you have no chance of bluffing Drunky-tilty in this spot. You need some kind of hand to win here, so if you don't have one, get out. So what if he wins the hand or if someone else gets his last hundred? That money will still be there on the table for you to go after—assuming that you haven't crippled yourself in a reckless pursuit.

You know, even a fantasy can go both ways. Even in your imagination you might not succeed in driving the reraiser off his hand or showing down something better than Drunky-tilty's got. Well, that's the beauty of fantasy poker—the chips are fantasy too. The experience you gain, however, in constructing and analyzing the situation— that's completely real. That's something you can use.

I don't draw much distinction between fantasy and reality. It's my blessing or my curse to experience an invented situation almost as intensely as the real thing. Nevertheless, if I find myself in a live game that mirrors one of my fantasy constructions (which, after all, only mirror all the live games I've ever played in), I have the comforting sense of *no surprises here*. Thus I find that constructed fantasies have become a tool I can use to turn my idle poker musings into directed poker exercises.

Give it a whirl. Think about poker situations that vex you a great deal, then navigate a fantasy course through those situations where you're not vexed, but rather triumphant. You can even do it like a dialogue:

> "Okay, pop quiz: You're in the small blind with 9-8 suited. It's folded around to the button, where a notorious blind-stealer raises into you. What do you do?"
>
> "What are the limits?"
>
> "Five and dime."
>
> "Blinds?"
>
> "Two and five."
>
> "I fold. It's not worth it."
>
> "You're just going to let him run over you?"
>
> "9-8 suited is a drawing hand. I need more customers to justify my odds."
>
> "He's bluffing."
>
> "He has position."

"You're being weak."

"I'm being careful."

"If I were him, I'd come after you."

"I'd wait for a good hand and trap you."

"You try."

"I will."

"Good, that's a good attitude. You pass."

At minimum, this is *modeling positive behavior*. It will give you the strength of will to do the right thing when the situation demands. Even given the difference between fantasy and reality, if you can be unafraid in a fantasy, it's easier to be unafraid in reality, too. When fear moves out, tranquility moves in.

TRANQUILITY

Are you tranquil when you play poker? Are you calm and placid in your seat, with the keen concentration of a clear and focused mind? Or are you in turmoil, all sweats, squirms, and clenchy teeth? If you don't have tranquility in a poker game, obviously, you lose much to opponents who do, because their perceptions and decisions will remain crisp and unfiltered, while you will be perpetually perceptually clouded by your own anxiety.

Though it would be nice to say, "Never play poker when you feel fear," there's a problem with that, for a little fear is actually a healthy thing. Fear sends us fleeing, appropriately, from fire or flood. In poker, fear can keep us focused on playing our best game. This is why some high-limit players, as we've already noted, often do poorly in low-limit games: They have no fear. They can't possibly lose (or win) enough in this teeny game to make a difference. So they play without fear but also without caution. Sure they're fearless, but it's the wrong kind of fearless. It's "careless fearless" because the outcome doesn't matter.

> *You have to care about the outcome in order to play your best game.*

Doesn't it follow that if you care about the outcome, then you must fear bad outcomes? Not necessarily—not, certainly, if you are able to draw this distinction: Care about the outcome without becoming hooked on the outcome. *Want* to win, *desire* to win, *strive* to win—but don't *need* to win in order to feel good about yourself.

As we've already established, there's a definable dollar limit for each of us where the money matters, but doesn't matter so much as to take us outside our comfort zone. If you play consistently at this limit, you can play consistently with tranquility, and even lose with tranquility (though, of course, you have no intention of losing). This leaves you free to concentrate on the only thing that matters: playing your best game. Win or lose, if you can walk away from the table confident that you did your best, then you are detached from outcome. Consequences no longer matter to you. Only performance matters now.

> *In the presence of fear, nothing is possible; in the absence of fear, everything is possible.*

Therefore you must come to the table fear-free. Though not—again the critical distinction—care-free. Have the commitment to play perfect poker plus the tranquility to accept bad outcomes.

You will not be surprised to discover, I'm sure, that this commitment plus this tranquility actually trends you toward good outcomes and away from bad ones. Your commitment to perfect poker keeps you from making bad plays, the kind of bonehead nonsense that costs you plenty when you're just screwing around. Your tranquility in the face of possible adverse outcomes will help you make the most (through fearless aggressive betting) of situations where you have the best of it. Further, your utter detachment from outcome will keep you from going on tilt when luck, such as it is, turns against you.

Do I imagine that you have become a charming little Buddha, sitting lotus-like in your seat, keeping your head while all those around you are losing theirs? *You bet your Buddhist little butt I do!* If I found you in that perfectly calm, perfectly Zen state of mind, I would be perfectly terrified of playing against you and perfectly justified in feeling that way. So come on, impress me with your peace of mind. Fold your ragged blind hands in the face of a raise, no matter how long it's been since you've played a hand. Get away from your pair of queens when the board comes A-K-x and a raising war breaks out. Muck your hand with grace when some muttonbird draws thin to a flush that gets there on the river.

Or, on the other hand, doubt me, foolish doubter. Tell me that you think it's the hotheads who prosper in poker because their hot heads give them the table presence required to dominate the game. *Maybe*, I reply. A hothead *image* can be very effective. A hothead *reality* is something altogether different. Look around the next table you play at, and consider the state of mind of the big winners. Are the players with the tall stacks all stressed out and apprehensive? "Of course, they're not stressed out," you reply, "they've got the tall stacks!" I say you have it exactly backward: They've got the big stacks because they're not stressed out. They're free from worry, and thus free to concentrate on their game.

The logic of this quickly starts to chase its own tail: *To achieve, seek not to achieve.* In order to be a winner, you have to be calm. In order to be calm, you have to be free from fear. In order to be free from fear, you have to disconnect from the need to be a winner. You succeed, in sum, by not trying to succeed. How confusing is that?

Confusion, though, is the start of understanding, so here's the conundrum unraveled: Measure success in process, not product. Have perfect process and you'll have success, regardless of the size of your stack. It just so happens that perfect process leads to large stacks, but that's merely a residual benefit of playing clear-headed poker in a tranquil, peaceful state.

> *Next time you play poker,* **don't stack your chips.** *Don't let yourself know how many you have. And when you go to cash out,* **don't.** *Take your chips home in a paper bag and bring them back uncounted to your subsequent session. In this way you'll give yourself an object lesson on the difference between money and chips: Chips are what we use to play Killer Poker. Money is just something we spend.*

SCRIPTS

People often play poker according to given patterns of behavior. We've all played against players in negative moods and against players in positive moods. Sometimes the behavior is conscious and sometimes it's unconscious. What makes these people tick?

Obnoxious Players

To an asshole, the whole world looks dark. Over and over again at the poker table we encounter rude, obnoxious, glower poker players who don't seem to be having a good time no matter how well they're running. These players boggle the mind, do they not? They whine loudly about every bad beat and curse profoundly any dim innocent who happens to draw out on them.

To an asshole, the whole world looks dark. For players like these, glum is just their standard state of mind. They're glum when they wake up, glum over morning coffee, glum through their workday, glum on the freeway, and glum when they get to the club. Even their wins have no power to please them. Even the satisfaction of playing properly doesn't move them off their dour negativity. If they get lucky, they figure it's only a matter of time before the poker gods look their way and start punishing them again.

> "What's the difference between an optimist and a pessimist?"

> "An optimist looks at the glass and says it's half full. A pessimist looks at the glass and says, 'If I drink this, I'll spill it all over myself and ruin my shirt.'"

So then, one must wonder, why do the assholes play poker at all, since it so manifestly does nothing to relieve the ongoing assholity of their life's experience? The answer, I believe, lies in *scripts*.

What Are Scripts?

Scripts are the patterns of behavior that we humans use to organize and run, or sometimes enslave, our lives. Some of these scripts are dark, subconscious, and toxic. Other scripts are strategies, battle plans devised in advance and executed thoughtfully at the appropriate moment. Your success or failure as a poker player depends largely on which type of scripts you play.

I almost said, "type of scripts you *choose* to play," but then I changed my mind, because a lot of times you don't have a choice about your scripts. If they're sufficiently hidden, then you play them whether you like it or not.

Toxic Scripts

Any time you're on tilt for example—for even a moment—you're playing a toxic script, the "I don't deserve my rotten fate" script. Instead of playing to win, you're playing for payback against the drunken bozoid who just gave you a bad beat, to get back to even, or to assuage pain with a quick, recovering win.

It's a toxic script when you defend a blind you shouldn't, just because you're tired of some loudmouth blowhole taunting you while he pushes you off your hand. It's a toxic script when you call with J-5 just because you're bored. It's a toxic script when you bet the ponies or the baseball game, just because the poker game you're in isn't providing sufficient stimulation to meet your current needs.

What other toxic scripts do you play? Can you be frank enough to declare them to yourself in your notebook or at least in your mind?

- I play to impress others with my prowess.
- I'm a jerk on purpose.
- I belittle other players or dealers just to inflate my sense of self.
- I let my impatience get the best of me.
- I blow off steam with bad language.
- I make loose calls just for the sake of being in the action.

What else?

- _____
- _____
- _____
- _____

Toxic scripts play out on a larger level, too. Your whole decision to play poker on a given day, for example, can be a toxic script. "I had a lousy day at work today, and man am I gonna take it out on those flakes at the club. Someone's gonna get punished, you betcha!" That's a *revenge* script, but notice that it's not even revenge against the real enemy. That designation would go to whomever or whatever in your life made you mad enough to play revenge poker in the first place. It's a given: You're not going to resolve nonpoker issues by playing poker; yet every day people try.

The most toxic script—the *loser* script—is one that touches the deepest psychology of some players. I hope you're not a victim of this script because if you are, then you're probably not a happy person to begin with, let alone a successful or proficient poker player, and my heart goes out to you. Here's how that bad thing happens:

People have worldviews, opinions of the reality around them. In defense of their worldview, some people will do anything in their power to get outer reality to conform to their beliefs. Some sad people, it happens, have been taught from an early age (by flawed parents or other adults) that they are losers or victims and they deserve to fail. You'd think they'd go out of their way to avoid reinforcing this negative worldview, but they don't. Because even if outer reality confirms a negative worldview, it still *confirms* that worldview and, on the gut level, makes the person holding that worldview feel valid and good—reassured that the world is, if not an uplifting place, at least a conforming one.

As already noted, the poker world is peopled with such compulsive losers. Seen now in terms of their scripts, we can understand that they're feeding a certain addiction, the specific addiction of feeling good about feeling bad.

Positive Scripts

Enough negativity! The issue here is *positive scripts,* strategies and tactics you use or can use to refine and polish your game.

Some scripts are general: "Today I will play selectively aggressive poker." Some scripts are situation-specific: "I will find players who routinely call the flop but fold the turn and make it a point to bet through them." Some scripts are ad hoc responses to situations as they evolve: "That guy bluffs too much. I'll look for a spot where I can lay back and trap him." Some scripts are just prescriptions for appropriate or useful behavior. "I'll study a poker book for half an hour before I go to play today." And some scripts have a Zen feel: "I'll play right now."

All of these scripts are positive scripts because they address the question of "How can I play better poker?" rather than buying into the question of "How can I feel better (or less bad) about myself?"

I'm sure you appreciate the distinction between positive and negative scripts. Positive scripts are conscious, present, alive, dynamic, and conducive to good play. Negative scripts are lurkers, designed to sabotage behavior for the sake of ego or worldview.

Can you eradicate negative scripts from your play? Not completely, but you can bury your negative scripts in an avalanche of positive ones. Remove toxic toeholds for your negative scripts simply by using positive ones to push them aside.

Suppose you have a "tilt" script that's giving you problems. Replace it with a script that says, "Emulate tilt; act like you're on tilt, but don't be." Then, in situations where you'd normally fall into tilt behaviors, you'll have a strong counterprogram to keep you on track. You'll fall into tilt-masquerade behaviors instead. It may look like tilt to your opponents, but you'll know it's not, and you'll prosper accordingly.

Or here's another example. Remember that asshole we talked about, the one who directs his fury at any sad lumpkin who draws out on him? Have you ever played that script? If you have, then you know that it momentarily feels good, because it momentarily salves your psychic ache. You also know that it's bad for you in the long run, because if you make the lumpkins feel unloved, they'll either improve or go away, and either way you don't get their money. So if you've got a temper going, and you find yourself at risk for abusing weak players, substitute a "killing with kindness" script instead. Next time some fool draws out on you with slim odds, make a point of positively reinforcing his negative draw. Take pride in how well you can take the beat in stride. This will keep your temper in check and also keep the mook and his money at the table.

To understand the impact of positive and negative scripts on your poker, you have to see them in the context of your true self. That's impossible for many people and difficult for most. If you're lost or confused (or a little bit afraid) remember this simple shorthand:

> *Positive scripts serve your poker, negative scripts serve your ego; positive scripts are about thinking your poker, negative scripts are about feeling it.*

If you engage your mind in a detailed and thorough examination of your mind, you can expect to derive benefits far outside the realm of poker. Once you learn to interpret all of your actions in terms of positive and negative scripts, you might find yourself free of some angers and resentments that have long stood between you and a happy life.

Does inefficiency drive you nuts? If you encounter a dealer doing a poor job, does it put you on a precariously short fuse? Understand that when you unleash your impatience in the form of anger, you end up hurting two people. Obviously you hurt the dealer, who may very well be doing the best he can, and in any case doesn't deserve to have your vitriol hurled in his face. Also you're hurting yourself, because your anger boomerangs back on you in terms of *a bad mood*. How can you have a good day if you're mad at the world? How can you play quality poker?

You may think that going from angry and impatient to temperate and placid is too global a change for your personality to manage. Well, you're right—you can't be completely transformed in an instant—but you can make a lasting commitment to change, and you can engineer the success of that commitment merely by changing the style and substance of the scripts you play. Try it. It's better for the world, better for poker, and better for you.

> *Now that you know what script-driven behavior is, make it a point to identify what scripts your opponents are playing. Positively scripted players should be avoided; negatively scripted players should be savagely attacked.*

The Bad Beat Script

I think that one of the most harmful scripts a poker player can play is the "bad beat" script. This is where you tell a fellow player how the universe did you wrong, in hopes that the fellow player can somehow use his authority with the universe to undo the damage done to you. The telling of bad beat stories has become so annoying as to devolve into cliché. In certain circles, if you tell someone a bad beat story, you have to give them a dollar. That's something of a joke, of course, but beneath every joke there is an underlying truth and pain. In this case, the truth is, "This person is telling me something I don't care about," and the pain is, "There's not a damn thing I can do about it except listen politely, what a drag."

Of course, for the person receiving the bad beat, and telling the bad beat story, the underlying truth and pain are something altogether different.

BEATS

There are no bad beats, only temporary setbacks. Against an opponent I identify as a total woodentop (oak from the neck up) I raise pre-flop with K-K. The flop comes K-x-x with one club. He calls all the way and catches two more clubs to beat me with 8-4 suited. I don't even bother to wonder why he called in the first place. Some people just do.

So here's the news:

> *There are no bad beats, only temporary setbacks.*

A few hands later, the very same player calls to the river with the idiot end of the straight, and I get all my bets back and then some. This just demonstrates that blind luck may be lucky, but it's blind just the same. Eventually the bad play of bad players will cost them everything they have.

In the meantime, *there are no bad beats, only temporary setbacks.* Against an opponent I don't know very well, I watch the board pair on the river and then watch my opponent check disconsolately. I bet—and he raises, taking the pot with a late-blooming full house. He has fooled me with a false tell. Absolutely sucked me in. Yes, he caught a card on the river to set up the play, but who fell into his trap? Me. That was me. I got spanked, and deservedly so. This is not a bad beat. This is an opportunity to learn about my opponent and learn from my mistakes. The only real question is: Will I?

There are no bad beats, only temporary setbacks. A beat only turns bad when you use it as a weapon against yourself—when, for example, you use a bad beat as permission to go on tilt. Your (il)logic runs this way: "If good cards can't win; maybe bad cards can."

There are no bad beats, only temporary setbacks. There was a hold'em tournament once that had the following wrinkle: Five players out of 150 had $100 bounties on their heads—a very high bounty, considering that the tournament buy-in was also $100. One marked man went all-in, and the player to his left drew a bead on that juicy bounty with the pocket aces he felt extremely fortunate to be holding in that situation. He figured to have a lock when the flop came A-9-9. Can you guess how the story ends? Our hero lost the pot and the bounty when the all-in player turned over, yep that's right, pocket nines. These things happen. They happen all the time.

About that time, a friend of our hero came over, having just busted out of the tournament. Although our hero had a legitimate (and really interesting) bad beat story to tell, the friend wasn't listening. At that moment, the friend was in so much pain from having busted out of the tournament that he just had to yammer on and on about his bad beat, just to get some relief from the sorrow and remorse he felt.

You learn a lot about the human condition by watching

how people treat their beats. The friend, of course, was already out of the tournament, having played himself out of it, I have no doubt. But our hero recovered from his stunning reversal and crawled all the way to the final table. Let's all say it together, shall we? *There are no bad beats, only temporary setbacks.*

You can avoid some bad beats just by not doing stupid things. Why would you want to call a raise with 9-5 offsuit ever? So you can catch top pair and a poor straight draw when the flop comes 9-8-7? Only to lose to a ten when your six hits on the river? So you can then bleat *bad beat, bad beat*? That's not a bad beat; that's bad play.

The minute we get lucky we get loose, and it's almost always a mistake. If you're running well, you probably have a good image, "a don't mess with me because you can't possibly outthink me or outplay me" image. You do want to press your edge, of course, but you don't want to squander it on meaningless reckless weak adventures. Sure you can raise with A-6, but the first time you get called down and outkicked (by someone playing a sensible A-Q) you lose all the perceived invincibility you had held. Why would you want to do that?

Poker is so simple. Really, truly it is. You don't have to be a great player or even a good player—just better than bad players, and that's not hard. Man, that's easy. Some players are so bad that almost any time they act it's a mistake. You can beat them—as long as you don't sink to their level.

Just expect them to get lucky every now and then—because they will—and don't bemoan your fate when they do. *There are no bad beats, only temporary setbacks.* If bad players didn't ever get lucky, they couldn't ever play, and if they couldn't ever play, you couldn't ever take their money away—and that would be a bad beat indeed!

> *Any time you lament your fate, you betray*
> *weakness—emotional weakness—and your*
> *strongest foes stand ready to stomp all over*
> *you for that. Got a bad beat story? At all cost,*
> *keep it to yourself!*

Top Ten Ways I'm Dumb at Poker

If someone tells you they're smarter than you, they are, in fact, not. If they were smarter than you, they'd know better than to tip you off to that fact, and thus put you on your guard. If they were truly smart, they wouldn't want to make you feel inferior because then you might get grumpy and not give them what they want. With that in mind, far be it from me to claim to be smarter than anyone. In fact, let me underscore the point by listing the Top Ten Ways I'm Dumb at Poker. I figure if I, Mr. In-Print Poker Author, can admit my tragic flaws, you should be able to admit yours too—no matter how smart or dumb we all are.

   10. *I get cocky when I get ahead.* Many are the winning sessions I've turned into losing sessions by confusing good fortune with good play. A few key cards can make the difference between booking a win and booking a loss. If I always remembered this fact, my own hubris would not get the best of me.

   9. *I take slim draws.* It's amazing how I can miscompute the simple math of a draw when ego is at stake. I *know* I only have a four-outer, but I will jump through any mental hoops necessary (visions of implied odds dancing in my head) in order to justify the draw.

   8. *I get glowery when I get behind.* Not that I'd ever come right out and be rude, but I do tend to withdraw into a shell when things aren't going my way. There's nothing

wrong with turning tight when the situation demands, but my best style is gregarious and flamboyant, so the silent, withdrawn me is not my strongest version.

7. *I push a rush too far.* Related to getting cocky when I get ahead, I can't always consolidate my gains without giving at least some of them back. This is often a case of overestimating my table strength or table image. Just because I'm hitting my hands doesn't necessarily mean the other players will fear me and start backing down.

6. *I lack stamina or focus.* After a few hours of playing poker, especially in tournaments, attention deficit disorder kicks in and my mind starts to wander. It may be that I'm just not cut out for monomaniacal marathon poker. I like to do too many other things.

5. *I fear losing money.* No matter how many times I tell myself that it's only chips and that outcomes don't matter, I still can't let go of the fear of losing all that . . . value. When I'm within my comfort range, I'm fine, but when I put, gee, a mortgage payment on the table, I start to get a little frayed around the confidence.

4. *I stay in bad games.* Either through inertia, pride, or denial, I can often convince myself that a game isn't really as bad as it is. Despite the evidence of my eyes, I can persuade myself that my opponents are not as frisky, tricky, deceptive, or clever as they clearly manifest themselves to be. Leaving a bad game is a sign of intelligence, not cowardice.

3. *I don't complete my drives.* Good players can raise pre-flop, bet the flop, bet the turn, bet the river, and eventually drop all opposition. I *know* that they don't have the hands they're representing all the time. What they have is the essential ability to drive their bluffs home. I will frequently break off a drive, checking the turn and the river if I haven't dropped the field by then. Maybe I'm convinced

that I won't get all my opponents to fold, but maybe I am not right.

2. *I let myself get mooked by false tells.* Many is the time I have bet into a check-sigh, only to find myself facing a check-raise where I expected to get a check-fold or a crying call. In these cases, my foe's bad acting conspires with my own greed to trap me into trying to extract extra value where there is none to be had.

And the number one thing I do wrong:

1. *I loosen up.* I loosen up when I'm winning. I loosen up when I'm losing. I loosen up when I'm tired or agitated or bored. I start out playing squeaky tight, but soon find myself turning the handle just a notch or two counterclockwise. Next thing I know, the valve is all the way open and I'm playing every cockamamie hand I can get my hands on. I think I'm being frisky, but I'm really just out of line.

To my credit, there are a few common mistakes that I don't make. I don't buy in short, ever. I don't rebuy when I rack off badly, ever. I don't blame bad luck or bad karma for bad outcomes, ever. I don't berate dealers or other players, ever. I don't ask for deck changes or new setups, ever. I don't gamble more than I can stand to lose, ever. I don't get angry, ever (except angry with myself for manifestly mullet-headed plays; but I get over it quick). I don't play drunk, ever.

At this point you may be thinking that you're smarter than I am because you don't make any of the errors I make. Maybe you don't, but I'm betting that there are some serious errors you *do* make. I'm further betting that you know *exactly* what they are. So write those down in your notebook, even at the risk of repeating observations you've already made. Repetition is good for us—it's how we learn.

Also write down the errors you *never* commit, because, hell, you deserve to feel good about your play, and you deserve to acknowledge and give yourself credit for the things you do right.

No one plays flawlessly forever. It's a goal we pursue but not an end we can achieve. In pursuit of perfect poker, I find that it helps to be *patient* and *impatient* at the same time. I'm patient with myself in the sense that I'll forgive my mistakes but impatient with myself in the sense that I'm determined not to make them again. In the end, I think, that's all anyone can ask—even the players who are smarter than us.

SNAKEBIT

Bad outcomes can leave you talking to yourself. That's not a huge problem unless you start talking to other people, too, for the obvious reason that it reinforces the notion that you're a loser and a schmuck. Why would you want any of your dangerous foes thinking *that*? While you're talking to yourself, make sure you talk about the right thing: not what happened last; rather, what happens next.

Okay, here's the situation. You start with a big pocket pair, flop a set, and drive it just like you should. Some shopping cart calls and calls and calls with an inferior holding, and catches a two-card 23-1 shot to make a flush on the river to take you down. You're sad; you shouldn't have lost that pot and you know it. No wonder you're talking to yourself.

Then comes the next hand, and a shot at redemption. It's not quite as good as a big pocket pair—let's say A-Q suited—but definitely worth a raise, especially since your recent bad beat can make it look like a tilt raise. So much so that five people call. Flop comes Q-6-3, and you start to feel like the odds are evening out. You bet and get called in three spots. The turn brings a king, but you're damned if you'll slow down now, so you fire off a bet.

Someone raises. Oh, dear. Now would be an excellent time to get away from this hand, but you don't because you believe in equal parts that first, the raiser's just playing with you, and second, if there's any justice you'll catch the river card you need. The river's a brick and you check-and-call, staring in numb stupefaction at the chowderhead's inevitable K-Q. What bad luck! You're snakebit for sure.

Who did the biting on that hand? Was it your foe who called your intended-to-look-like-tilt raise pre-flop, flat-called the flop with his top pair, good kicker, and then took over the hand on the turn? I don't think so. I think that the one doing the biting of you was you. Sad story, but typical. You got beaten by that flush on the hand before, and sure that was a bad beat. Then you lost control of this hand *because you were still thinking about the last hand!* You could have gotten away from this hand when you were raised on the turn, but you didn't. You refused to believe you'd been snakebit two hands in a row.

Well, okay, all it cost you was a couple of big bets. It's not the end of the world—unless the back-to-back snake-bites now turn around and start biting you all over.

You pick up your next cards—pocket fives—and decide that they're good for a raise (they'll really think you're steaming now!—Because, chucklehead, you *are*). When the flop comes *sans cinc* you try to run a bluff, which, of course, doesn't work because there's an ace on the flop and at least a couple of good aces out there. Now you're actually *hoping* for your *own* long shot to hit and get you out of this mess. When it doesn't happen, you think that you're worse than snakebit, you're cursed, and since you're cursed, there's no point in even *trying* to play correctly. On the next hand—oh, hell, it doesn't matter what happens on the next hand. Your discipline is gone. Your concentration is kaput. Your positive mental attitude is in shreds. You're angry, anxious, antsy, and depressed. *How can you play poker?*

Well, you can't. All you can do is swallow your loss, walk away, and try to find some recovery for your game.

Recovery

Recovery is an interesting word. Alcoholics in recovery have a little saying they use, called the Serenity Prayer. It gives them strength when things go bad, and you might use it when you're feeling snakebit.

> God, grant me the serenity
> to accept the things I cannot change,
> the courage to change the things I can,
> and the wisdom to know the difference.

Serenity to accept the things I cannot change. When you get smacked by a turn-and-river flush draw, *accept that you lost the hand!* Don't compound your error by believing that what happened should not have happened, and that you can somehow undo the damage by what you do next. You can't undo the damage; you can only make things worse.

Courage to change the things I can. The last hand doesn't matter. Only the next hand matters. If you have the courage to play proper poker in the face of bad outcomes, then you have a chance to pull out of this mess. If the next hand comes as junk—*treat* it as junk. Don't compound someone's bad beat by piling on a beat of your own. You deserve better than that.

Wisdom to know the difference. Sure, the turn-and-river catch was a bad beat, but what about that K-Q catch? Was that really a bad beat, or was it merely the result of an opponent taking your seeming tilt-raise at face value? Sure, you had the lead pre-flop, but most of the damage on that hand was purely self-inflicted. You can't call it a bad beat, because it isn't.

The Serenity Prayer is a marvelous tool for dealing with some extreme difficulties in life. It's no less marvelous for poker, so memorize it and recite it as a necessity to stabilize your play. It has gotten a lot of people through a lot worse problems than yours, but you can exploit it to make sure that the snake who bites you is, at minimum, someone other than you.

> *It's useful to have a mantra, something you can say to yourself to keep from going postal when things go bad. Some use the serenity prayer. Others use* there are no bad beats, only temporary setbacks. *Do you have a mantra? If not, invent one now. It never hurts to have some soothing words.*

6

♣ ♠ ♦ ♥

ODDS AND ODDS AND ENDS

♣ ♤ ◇ ♡

ODDS

I'm not a freak for odds. I'm not one of these guys who can tell you that you were 16.5-3 against picking up a redraw on the turn or completing your hand on the river or both (and aren't those guys just the most annoying people—especially after they've beaten you out of a pot?).

The truth is, I don't sweat the odds all that much. I prefer to exploit the big advantage offered in the differential between my skill and my opponents' skill rather than the sometimes-quite-slim edge offered by the odds qua odds. You don't have to be a freak for odds to be successful in poker, but it's useful to have the confidence that comes from knowing when the math, at least, is on your side, so let's take a look at some notable poker odds.

Odds, as we know, are really just fractions stated in reverse. If the odds, for example, are 2-1 against a certain outcome, this means that the event is likely to occur one time in three.

The odds you'll find here are *approximate* odds, rounded off to whole numbers (or in some cases half numbers).

Though the numbers are easier to grasp and therefore more useful this way, it does create some inconsistencies. Common sense tells us, for instance, that if there are eight cards that complete an open-ended straight and nine cards that complete a flush, they can't have identical hit-on-the-turn-or-river odds of 2-1. To which my response is (a) true, and (b) so what?

The point of knowing the odds is not to be an odds wonk but to be an informed bettor or caller. Whatever you're drawing to, you need pot odds in excess of card odds to justify your call. Whether you're 6.217-1 against completing or 5.932-1 against completing, it's a bad bet either way if you're only getting a 2-1 return on your investment. In most cases, approximate odds will do just fine.

In fact, you can tangle yourself up in odds. Knowing that the odds justify a call is not alone reason enough to make the call. Have you contemplated the possibility of your opponents hitting an even bigger hand? What if they're bluffing? Do you anticipate facing a reraise? Would a raise on your part drop all the competition right now? How about redraws? To me, odds represent the beginning of analysis, not the end.

So let's make it simple.

Card Odds and Pot Odds

When we speak of *card odds,* we're speaking of the chances of a certain outcome taking place, expressed as *odds against.* The card odds of picking up pocket aces are 220-1; on average, you'll have pocket aces once every 221 hands. When we speak of *pot odds,* we're speaking of the money that the pot is offering you for a given proposition. If you are fourth to act and three players have entered the pot in front of you, the pot is offering you 3-1 odds on your call. When poker players speak of *having the best of it,* they mean that the potential payoff for completing a hand is greater than the odds against doing so.

For example, say you have four to a flush in hold'em. Knowing that you need to complete your flush to win the pot, you contemplate calling a $20 bet before the river. There's $200 in the pot already, so the pot is offering you a *10-1* return on your $20 investment; *pot odds are 10-1.* Meanwhile, there are 9 flush cards unaccounted for out of 46 cards remaining in the deck. 9/46 = 0.1956521, a pretty much altogether useless number that we round off to the much more practical 20 percent; roughly one time in five you'll complete your draw. So that's *card odds* of one in five or 4-1 against. Since the pot odds are more than double the card odds, you have a clear call here.

Assuming that no one is drawing to a higher flush. Assuming that no one is drawing to a straight flush. Assuming that your flush card doesn't pair the board, giving someone else a full house or four of a kind. And assuming that a sudden tsunami doesn't sweep down on the card room and wash all the money away. Assuming, assuming, assuming. The road to poker hell is paved with odds assumptions.

So, again, let's make it simple:

Slim draws require big pots. Fat draws don't.

If you go with that rule of thumb, you won't go too far wrong, whether you can do an exact pot-odds-to-card-odds calculation on the fly or not.

Okay, starting with hold'em, here are some odds worth knowing.

HOLD'EM ODDS STARTING HANDS	
Hand	*Odds Against*
A-K suited	331-1
A pair of aces	220-1
A-K unsuited	110-1
A pair of jacks or higher	55-1
Suited cards 10 or higher	32-1
Any pair	16-1
Unsuited cards 10 or higher	10-1
A pair or an ace	4-1
Suited cards	3-1

One good thing about knowing the odds is that it under-cuts the debilitating sense of *entitlement* that so many of us take to the table. If you go all day without seeing suited A-K, for example, you start to think that you're owed, some-how—you're overdue, and you're owed good cards. Are you really? If you went *ten hours* without seeing that hand, your odds wouldn't be terribly outside the norm. So stop fretting over never getting premium hands. You get your fair share. Maybe you just don't recognize what your fair share is.

Beyond that, the odds give us clear, hard evidence of where our game is woefully out of line. Suppose we're thinking of defending our blind with weak suited cards against an early position raiser (or two!). What are we hop-ing for? Why, to flop a flush of course. The odds of that happening are *well over 100-1 against!* When are we ever going to get pot odds that justify taking a 100-1 shot? Never, that's when.

Also, don't get too excited about being dealt a pair. In a full game, about a third of the time someone else is likely to have been dealt a pair too. The lower your pair is, the greater the chance that that other pair dominates yours.

Also, get this: Since the odds of starting with a pair or an ace are only 4-1 against, if you *don't* start with a pair or an ace, you're likely facing *two* such hands in any full table situation. Kinda makes you feel less frisky about your 7-6 suited, doesn't it?

Now let's take a look at the likelihood of certain on-the-flop outcomes.

HOLD'EM ODDS
WHAT FLOPS MAY COME

Event	Odds Against
Flopping a flush	118-1
Flopping a set to two unpaired cards	73-1
Flopping two pair to two unpaired cards	48-1
Flopping a four-flush after starting suited	8-1
Flopping a set after starting with a pair	7.5-1
Flopping a pair to two unpaired cards	3-1

This chart throws some hold'em truths into pretty sharp relief. Contemplating again the odds against flopping a flush, you may find yourself wondering why you'd ever enter a pot on the strength of flush values alone. Sure, you might argue, your chances of flopping a flush are pretty slim, but your odds of flopping a flush *draw* are only 8-1 against. Yes, true—a draw that may or may not get there. The numbers don't lie. By itself, with no high-card or straight-card help, it's a *dumb draw*.

Another example: You're in the small blind, there's an early position raise and it's folded around to you. You hold T-9, and you know your foe well enough to put him on two big unpaired cards. You figure you'll be the favorite if you pair either of your cards, and you now know that that's a 3-1 shot. You're looking to put 1.5 small bets into a pot currently containing 3.5. Looking downstream, you see

that the big blind has no intention of calling. Too bad, because if you could count on him calling (assuming he
doesn't have a hand good enough to raise with) you'd get
clear odds to call. However, you don't let that stop you!
Even without the big blind's call, you figure that the pot
odds are close enough to the card odds to justify a call. If
the flop comes your way, you're in boss command!

The flop doesn't come your way, and it takes you a call
on the flop and a call on the turn to get that through your
head. Your crafty calculation of the odds has cost you five
small bets when you could've gotten away for half a bet
instead.

So here's how I suggest you use your knowledge of the
odds:

> *Let your knowledge of the odds give you a*
> *reason to* fold, *not to* call.

If you apply that rationale to your thinking, you're much
less likely to be seduced into making bad calls with what
could vaguely be considered adequate odds.

Implied Odds

Implied odds attempt to predict the money you can expect
to go into the pot on later rounds of betting. Contemplation of implied odds is crucial to your thinking. Without
implied odds, for example, you could never draw to a low
pair for a set.

You're thinking about calling with a pair of sevens. The
odds chart tells you that you're almost 8-1 against hitting
your set, and you see that the pot is only offering you 3-1
or 4-1. Fold, right?

Not necessarily. Considering your implied odds, you
may feel confident that *if* you hit your set and *if* it's the best

hand, or if you don't improve but still hold the best hand, *or* if you can bluff out your foes on the river, you will likely get several callers between here and there. All those callers—all those subsequent 3-1 and 2-1 returns on your single-bet investment—add up to implied odds in your favor.

Again, don't get carried away with implied odds, and always question your assumptions. Sometimes they'll all run scared. Sometimes you'll run into set-over-set situations. If all you think about are the numbers, the numbers will lead you astray.

Turning now to the turn and the river:

HOLD'EM ODDS
TURN AND RIVER

Drawing Hand	*Odds Against Completing on the Turn or River*
Three-card (runner-runner) flush draw	23-1
Full house draw with two pair	5-1
Full house draw with a set	2-1
Inside straight draw	5-1
Open-ended straight draw	2-1
Four-card flush draw	2-1

What this chart tells us at a glance is that if your hand is *mostly* complete on the flop, you're likely to get sufficient pot odds to continue. Again, the numbers can be misleading. Sure, you're only 2-1 against completing that flush or open-ended straight either on the turn or the river, but this assumes that you're going to call again if you miss your draw on the turn. You might even delude yourself into calling on the river if you happen to hit a pair or convince yourself that your foe is bluffing or something. Implied odds work both ways: They imply the money you could win, but also the money you could *lose*.

> *Use knowledge of the odds to avoid*
> *costly wishful thinking.*

The number that I consider most telling is that 23-1 runner-runner flush draw. You see people taking this draw all the time. They seem to get there a lot, but that's just our old friend confirmation bias again. The thing is, if you told some of these knuckleheads that they were 23-1 against completing the hand, they'd *still* take the draw. They didn't come here to *fold*, God love them, they came to *gamble*. So let them continue in blissful ignorance of the true odds; just don't let their unjustified optimism infect you too.

This also reinforces what we understand intuitively. When your crafty uncle who taught you poker told you, "Never draw to an inside straight," what he really meant was, "Rarely draw to an inside straight because you frequently won't find enough money in the pot or participants in the pot to justify your slim draw."

Don't neglect the vast difference between a call on the flop and a call on the turn. When you're drawing to an inside straight on the flop, your odds are roughly 5-1 against—not for that draw alone, but for that draw *combined* with another draw on the turn. In limit poker, it'll cost you two small bets to draw on the turn, and your odds against completing have roughly doubled, too. So you'll pay twice as much for an outcome that's half as likely.

Many players recognize this, so they'll take a shot at hitting their card on the flop, when it's "cheap" and then surrender their draw on the turn when the price of poker doubles. There's a problem with this thinking. If you know in advance that you're going to fold on the turn if you don't get there, then you're actually accepting a 10-1, not a 5-1, proposition when you call on the flop. Do the pot odds justify this call? Does the phrase *false economy* spring to mind?

By the way, if memorizing odds charts makes your head sweat, there's a quick-and-dirty shortcut you can use: Simply multiply your outs by the number of cards to come and then by 2 percent. Thus if there are eight cards that will complete your straight, and you have the turn and the river to try for them, that's $8 \times 2 \times 2$ percent, or 32 percent. Roughly 2-1 against, just like the chart says.

Say you're thinking about drawing to a two-outer on the river. Multiply two outs times one draw times 2 percent $(2 \times 1 \times 2)$. That's 4 percent or odds of 24-1 against. You'd better be staring at a *mound* of chips before you start considering that draw.

> *In the heat of battle, it's tough to calculate the odds no matter what method you use. So work on this skill when you're not in the hand. While ghosting other players, ask yourself, "If I were drawing to an inside straight and a backdoor flush, what kind of pot odds would I need to continue?" If you practice running the odds when you're not in the hand, you'll find it much easier to do when you are.*

Omaha/8 Odds

Many of your Omaha/8 odds decisions will be roughly equivalent to those you make in hold'em. For instance, if you're drawing to the nut flush on the river in hold'em, your chances of completing are 9/46 or 19 percent—call it 4-1 against. That same draw in Omaha/8 (assuming you have only two suited cards in your hand) is 9/44, or 20 percent, slightly higher because you've seen two extra nonsuited cards, but it's still roughly 4-1 against. You need roughly the same bunch of bets in the pot to make that call.

Or do you? You may, in fact, need *twice as big a bunch* of bets, because you may be shooting at only half the pot.

This is a typical error that the Omaholics typically make. They look at a board of, say A♥-J♥-9x-3x, and figure that their K♥-Q♥-x-x holding gives them a 4-1 draw at the nut flush. They count the bets already in the pot and make what they consider an easy call. Given, however, that seven of their nine hearts will complete a low, the bulk of their flush draw is probably only to *half* the pot. Worse, if the 9♥ or 3♥ comes, they're staring down the barrel of a possible full house. That means that there's exactly one card in the deck that gives them an absolute mortal lock on the whole pot. The T♥ . . . which completes a royal flush!

If you told them that their one-card draw to a royal was their only chance of winning the whole pot, would they think twice before jumping in? Of course, they would.

I know, I know, they have straight outs, they have half-pot outs; they may have backdoor outs in their other two cards. No wonder contemplation of the odds can lead to migraine headaches.

The Omaholics also tremble with excitement over hands like A-2 or A-2-3 because they know they're drawing to a lock for half the pot. How often does that draw actually get there? Let's look at some numbers.

	OMAHA/8 LOW DRAWS		
Holding	Times You'll Complete	Times You'll Complete If 2 Low Cards Flop	Times You'll Complete If 1 Low Card Flops
A-2	1 in 4	3 in 5	1 in 5
A-2-3	2 in 3	(roughly) 3 in 4	(roughly) 1 in 4
A-2-3-4	1 in 2	(roughly) 3 in 4	(roughly) 1 in 4

It may strike you as counterintuitive that you get there roughly as often with A-2-3 as with A-2-3-4. The key word is *roughly*—these numbers are rounded off to the nearest whole odds. In doing this round-off, we see that A-2-3 and A-2-3-4 are relatively close in strength. In other words, the fourth low card doesn't help you nearly as much as you might imagine.

Again, the odds are particularly useful in what they warn us against. That A-2 you're so excited about? It'll make a low a quarter of the time, yielding half the pot when it does. Sure it's a nut draw, but at the outset you're putting up $1 for an average win of 12.5 cents. How do you like that low draw now?

This is not to say that you shouldn't draw to nut low holdings in Omaha/8. To the contrary, the fact that you're drawing to a nut low (if it gets there) makes big low draws both attractive and profitable—*but you have to get there.* More often than not, if only one low card comes on the flop, we must muck our big fat low draw without sorrow or pity. The numbers tell us so.

Our hearts tell us otherwise, though, and that's where we get into trouble. To take another example, suppose you're holding 5-5-T-J and the flop comes 2-5-8. You like the fact that you've flopped a set, except that you're already playing for only half the pot—a pot that's likely to be driven hard by anyone holding a made low with a straight draw. Even if you do have the temporary nuts (which you may not—someone else could have a set of eights), you still have to survive dangerous turn and river cards—which *will* be either overcards, pair cards, or cards coordinated to low straight draws—in order to win *half* the pot.

This hand is a clear fold. Clear, at least, in light of the distressing math that underlies it. Many Omaha/8 players understand this hard reality—but then again, many don't, which is why Omaha/8 continues to play so profitably for those who do. If ever a game that beguiled its participants with wishful thinking, Omaha/8 is it. "All those *cards!* All those *combinations!* How can I not hit *something?"* Well, yeah, you will hit *something.* The question is *will you even make money when you hit?* The answer lies in numbers, not in foolish floptimism.

In Omaha/8, as in all flop games, you often have to make on-the-spot calculations of pot odds versus card odds. You want those calculations to be accurate, but you also don't want to tip off your observant foes that you're betting or calling with a draw as opposed to a made hand. Thus there is a certain need for speed with these numbers. So here's another quick-and-dirty shortcut, this one courtesy of Lee H. Jones, author of *Winning Low-Limit Hold'em.* Lee says:

> If you have fewer than ten outs, you can figure out the odds you need by dividing your outs into 40. For ten or more outs, divide your outs into 30 to get an estimate of your needed pot odds.

This is so neat it kills me that I didn't think of it myself. Say you've got pocket jacks and you're looking at a turn board of J-6-5-4. You're sure that someone has a made straight, so you'll need to improve your hand to win the pot. You have ten outs—a jack, three sixes, three threes and three fours—so you divide that number into 30 and get three. That means you have to see a total of three big bets already in the pot in order to make your call profitable. Most of the time you'll have plenty of overlay to justify the call—and now you have the math to feel justified in doing so.

To take another example, suppose you have an Omaha/8 hand like K-K-Q-Q. You're looking at a board of J-J-7-2 and you're pretty sure that one of your foes has a set of jacks. You need to hit one of your four outs (the four remaining kings and queens) to win. Dividing four into 40, you get ten, which means you need to be looking at a pot containing ten big bets in order to make the call. Here is one instance where you don't have to worry about playing for half the pot, since a hand that makes the low won't complete your hand anyway. Now all you have to do is make a rough count of the money in the pot and see if a call is warranted.

> *Keep track of the pot as it grows—not in terms of dollars or chips but in terms of betting units. If four players see the flop for one small bet each, think* two, *as in* two big bets present and accounted for now. *If you update this one number as the hand progresses, you'll have a handle on the pot odds when later-round betting decisions confront you.*

A lot of players don't get involved in calculating the odds at all—and many of them do just fine. They have a rough grasp of whether a call is warranted, and they'd rather not cloud their thinking, or slow down the natural movement of their bets, by stopping to ponder thin edges. On balance, if you're more or less right with the odds, you don't have to be too fine. Just make sure that you're not bucking the odds in a big way—calling with the worst of it—and you'll do all right.

Seven-Card Stud Odds

Here are some selected odds for the first three cards in seven-card stud:

**SEVEN-CARD STUD
START CHART**

Starting Hand	Odds
Three of a kind	424-1
A pair of aces	76-1
Three suited cards	18-1
Any pair	5-1

These are considered quality starting hands in seven-card stud. Other playable hands include (in certain circumstances) three to a straight and three unrelated high cards. It's interesting to note that in a typical eight-handed stud game, you'll find less than two players starting with so much as a pair on any average deal. This means that if you're holding a pair, you can make the assumption (until proven otherwise by opponents' aggressive betting) that yours is, if not the best hand, at least among the top two.

Of course, in most stud games, the bad hands are going to fold out of the way, leaving you isolated against quality competition. How likely are they, or you, to improve?

**SEVEN-CARD STUD
EVENTS AND OUTCOMES**

Starting Hand	Outcome	Odds
Three suited cards	Completing a flush	4.5-1
Three suited cards on fourth street	Completing a flush	8.5-1
Four suited cards on fourth street	Completing a flush	1.5-1
A pair	Making two pair	1.4-1
A pair	Making three of a kind or better	4.1-1
Three of a kind	Making a full house or better	1.5-1

This chart tells us what most stud players understand intuitively: If you don't improve on fourth street, you should probably fold. Just look at the difference between catching and not catching your fourth flush card. If you catch it, you're close to even money to complete your flush and will likely get generous pot odds to continue. If you don't catch your flush card on fourth street, you're climbing a hill of almost 9-1 against, and it's rare that a seven-card stud game is loose enough to offer pot odds sufficient to warrant that draw.

The chart also reveals how much more frequently you'll improve your pair to two pair than to three of a kind. It's useful, then, to ask yourself early and often whether two pair will be good enough to win a given pot, since it's the likeliest improvement you'll enjoy.

Finally—no surprise—your rare starting hand of trips rolled up is exactly the powerhouse you imagine it to be. Not only is it the best hand going in, it's almost even money to improve to a full house. Too bad we don't get them more often.

We could, of course, go much deeper into this. We could look at the precise odds of starting with two suited and connected cards and a pair, then improving to two pair, trips, a straight, a flush, a full house, quads, or a royal. After a certain point, though, the odds cease to be useful indicators and start to be crutches at best or impediments at worst. A basic knowledge of the card odds and a basic calculation against pot odds are usually enough for most situations. Anything beyond that, well, if it's of interest to you then go for it, but don't invest so much energy in your calculations that you pass a point of diminishing returns.

In all cases, beware of the real risk of misplacing the forest within a finely calculated number of trees. The point of knowing the odds is to *guide* your play, not *dictate* your play. Let your knowledge of the odds abet your card-reading ability, psychological aptitude, and other poker skills, and then you'll have the odds working for you—not against you.

To recap the main points:

1. A rough approximation is usually enough. The difference between 4.75 against and 5.1 against is insignificant if the pot ain't even offering 2-1.
2. Use shortcuts to do rough calculations, or keep track of the pot as it grows, or do both. Don't let your savvy opponents know that you're on a draw by pondering the odds too long.
3. Use the odds to justify *good* decisions, not *bad* ones. Use knowledge of the odds to avoid costly wishful thinking, and *don't* use imperfect knowledge of the odds to rationalize a call you know you shouldn't make.

> *If there are odds you* know *you need to know—such as the odds of completing certain hands in hold'em—practice with them like flashcards until you know them cold. Having memorized them once, you'll never have to fuss with them again.*

SCORECARD

Some people hate to keep score. "It's not whether you win or lose," they say, "it's how you play the game." In poker, however, you won't know how you played the game unless you keep track of the score. Of course, there's no perfect correlation between playing great poker and winning big bucks. Sometimes great players lose money and sometimes terrible players get terribly lucky and book big wins. Over time, there's simply no way to tell whether your poker game is any good *unless you keep score.*

Odds and Odds and Ends 205

Many players insist they don't need to. Ask them and they'll tell you, "Well, I don't keep track, but I'm sure I've won more than I lost." Know what? They're lying. They're lying to you, they're lying to the universe, and most of all they're lying to themselves. They don't keep score because they can't bear to face facts. Show me a poker player who refuses to track his wins and losses and I'll show you a poker player who has lost more—probably much more—than he's won. Not keeping score may be fine for sandlot softball, but it has no place in Killer Poker.

Not everyone can write the truth of his experience. Hell, not everyone can even *face* the truth of his experience. One of the secondary benefits I hope you've gotten from this book is the willingness to commit to paper true words about yourself and about how you play poker. I hope you've discovered that those words, in their frankness, do not hurt you, but rather help you by clarifying where your game is strong and where your game needs work. If you haven't been able to make this leap into writing, or even list making, well, it may be that you genuinely have no talent for words. That's fine. I have no talent for ice dancing or hitting a sandlot softball.

But even if you can't write words, you can still write numbers. So now we come to records: your poker scorecard.

No poker player can even start to call himself serious-minded unless he keeps track of his performance over time. If he fails to keep track, it's not laziness, it's denial and fear. Many players make the conscious or unconscious decision not to keep score because they know, deep in their gut, that they're not the winning players they intend or pretend to be, and it's easier for them to maintain their denial if they don't put contrary evidence right before their eyes.

If you can face this evidence, you'll find it very revealing, though it may take a long time for a true picture to emerge, because you can't trust short-term results. Anyone can catch a run of hot cards and end up mistaking good fortune for good play. An artificially inflated bankroll can delude you into thinking that you're better than you are, but detailed and meticulous records don't lie. If they tell you that you have lost twenty consecutive sessions of $30–$60 hold'em, there's hard evidence that you need to try a different limit or a different game or both.

How long is a long time? At what point does your statistical history start to become statistically valid? The answer depends on such factors as how much you play, how long your sessions are, and whether you play many different games, or many different limits, or both. (One bad session at $20–$40, for example, can wipe out 20 hours of diligence at $4–$8.) I would say this: Keep solid records for a solid year before worrying about the bottom line. Even if you're running red at the end of that year, it doesn't necessarily mean that you're a congenital loser. It just means you have some holes to fill.

Keeping records is not just about measuring the size of your stack over time. It's a tool for analysis, a way to figure out where you do well, where you do poorly, and why. Based on what you learn from studying your own stats, you can start to make better choices about where, when, what, and how to play.

For instance:

- Your records indicate that you win at $9–$18 but lose at $6–$12. Why might that be? The players are the same caliber—hell, the players are mostly the same people. The cards are the same, the club is the same, even the rake is the same, so—hang on— "even the rake is the same?" The $6–$12 game is two-thirds the size of the $9–$18 game, which means that, all other things being equal, you're only going to win two-thirds as much money, but the two different limits cost exactly the same amount to play. Hmm—moral of the story, stick to $9–$18, where your skills have a better chance of neutralizing the rake.

- Your win rate is higher in Omaha/8 than in hold'em, but your fluctuation is also much greater. This could be a function of your Omaha/8 opponents having more gamble in them than the hold'em foes you face. Whatever the reason, this information will warn you off playing Omaha/8 when your bankroll is running low.
- You do better in short sessions than in long ones. So quit before you're tired or your concentration flags.
- You do better at the Popsicle Club than you do at the Progress Casino. This one's easy: Play at the Popsicle.

This is the kind of information you can expect to extract from complete and meticulous records. Information is power; we know this. It's power you won't have unless you give it to yourself. What other sorts of insights can you expect to glean from your scorecard?

- Do I win more (or lose less) during the day or evening or dead of night?
- How do I rate in sessions where I stop in after work?
- How do I fare on poker vacations?
- Am I steady or streaky: Do I have small or large numbers of losses or wins in a row?
- Do I have many small losses and a few big wins or the other way around?

- How do my online and live game win rates compare?
- How does my home-game performance stack up to my card room results?

A caveat: Just as an overly enthusiastic appraisal of the odds can lead you to some bad decisions, an imperfect assessment of your own records can easily lead you to some false conclusions. Suppose your year-end review revealed that you did great in the clubs but got killed in home games. Does that mean you should give up on your home games? Maybe—or maybe it means that you need to look for hidden factors. Do you play looser in home games because you're "with friends"? Quitting may not be the answer; rather, let the numbers guide you toward ways to fine-tune your approach.

Or suppose that your records indicate that you just don't do well on road trips. You're fine in your hometown, but when you go to Las Vegas, Atlantic City, or Tunica, your win rate tumbles. You might speculate that you're playing unusually long sessions during those getaways or that you're playing your "vacation" game rather than your normal "vocation" game. You might even blame your poor performance on the fact that you can drink while you play because you need only to stagger upstairs to a hotel bed and not have to drive home drunk. Are you going to stop taking road trips? Of course not. So you'd better use the information appropriately—not to stop playing, but to figure out how to play better.

Here's a simple three-step method for using your poker records effectively.

1. Accumulate data.
2. Interpret data.
3. *Act!*

Act—but act appropriately. If your records indicate that you're doing fine at $15–$30 but having trouble showing a profit at $30–$60, it doesn't mean *give up on moving up*. It means sit down and think about the $30–$60 game (maybe even just railbird it for a few hours instead of playing at all) and figure out what adjustments you need to make. Nobody's talking about giving up. We're just talking about making better-informed choices.

By the same token, don't become complacent if your numbers show that you're doing quite well. You may be playing excellent poker—or you may just be experiencing a run of hot cards. If you're winning, fine; take pride in your performance. Then *analyze* that performance and find out what you're doing best of all. Is game selection your strength? Knowing when to quit? If you're doing something very well, *do more of that.*

In all events, don't let your records become a burden to your soul. Awareness of the fact that you're running red can cause you to press, stress, and play even worse. Who needs that? Poker is supposed to be profitable, but it's also supposed to be fun. Don't let your past defeats—whether last week or last month or last year—keep you from playing your best game and enjoying the game you play, today. Twenty years from now, you won't remember this week's—or even this year's—results; so don't sweat what doesn't need to be sweated.

> *Use your records to* **inform** *yourself, not to* **judge** *yourself. If you do this, you'll be using your scorecard appropriately.*

If you're already keeping detailed records, keep doing what you're doing. If you're not yet keeping records, *start now*. Start with your very next session, and never let yourself slip. There may be bad news there, but it's better to have that news and acknowledge it than to let denial infect your play. All serious poker players keep records; all you have to do to call yourself serious is to keep records too.

As a secondary benefit, the records you keep will help you justify your keen interest in poker to those around you. If they say, "Geez, cowboy, you seem to be spending an *awful* lot of time playing poker," you can answer, "Well, that's true. Last year I played 205.5 hours of poker, at an average win rate of $9.75 per hour. So, yeah, I'm playing a lot of poker, but I'm making it pay for itself. Can you say the same about your ormolu clock collection?" Even if you have to cop to a losing record, at least you can cop to a full and complete losing record. At least you're not in denial.

So what kind of records should you keep? How should you go about it? Many players track nothing more than the number of hours played and the number of dollars won or lost. As a crude answer to the question, "Am I a net-plus player?" I suppose that's sufficient, but with so many other interesting questions to ask, why stop there?

More and more players these days carry Personal Data Assistants and enter all relevant information into their PDAs right there at the table. If that's a little too wonky for you, you might consider photocopying and using the following template on page 211.

You can use this form, or one like it, to transport your results from the club to your permanent records. I don't really care whether you keep your permanent records scrawled on a piece of old parchment or burned into a CD, but I will say this: With so many fine record-keeping programs available, why would you bother doing the math by hand? Use the best available tools; you can bet your competition is.

So then an excerpt from your play log might look something like the one on page 212.

Date	Club	Game Type	Limit	Time In	Hours Played	Buy-In	Profit (Loss)	Notes

JV'S PORTABLE SCORE SHEET AND HANDY DANDY SESSION LOG

JV'S PORTABLE SCORE SHEET AND HANDY DANDY SESSION LOG

Date	Club	Game Type	Limit	Time In	Hours Played	Buy-In	Profit (Loss)	Notes
2/8	Popsicle	Hold'em	$6–$12	1 pm	2.5	$200	($200)	Racked off and went home
2/11	Progress	Omaha/8	$6–$12/ kill	8:30 pm	10	$400	$120	Not much to show for an all-nighter
2/12	Progress	Hold'em	Pot limit	7 pm	3	$1,000	($600)	After last night I should've taken the day off
2/18	Home game	Dealer's choice	$5–$10	7 pm	5.5	$200	$600	Thank heaven for the home game

Beyond net results, the most useful column in this template is the *notes* column. It gives you a chance to record things you did particularly right or particularly wrong, or to describe extenuating circumstances. For instance, you might have had a $500 win, but you know that most of your profit came from one or two hands where the pots were huge and you happened to catch the cards you needed. A simple, humble "got lucky" in the *notes* column will help you keep your head on straight when evaluating your own results.

Sometimes you'll have a session so bad, both in terms of the way you played it and the results you got, that you'll be tempted to pretend that the session never existed. Don't give into that urge! You'll skew your results to the point where you'll never be able to trust them. Always record your outcomes honestly, fully, and faithfully—and don't sweat it when you run red. By keeping honest records, you keep your self-respect, and that fact—owning your own self-respect—is bound to make you a better player over time.

RECESS

Let's take a break, shall we?

Anagrams

Back in the early 1990s, when I was writing for *Card Player Magazine*, I used to pen a little column called "Notes from the Nervous Breakdown Lane." During that time, I became infatuated with anagrams, those demonic reshufflings of a name or group of words that reveal the mystic or humorous hidden significance of that name or that group of words. Thus I discovered that Mike Caro was *okra mice*, and Tony

Holden was *holy tendon*, and Max Shapiro was *aphorism ax*, and Roy West was *rosy wet*, and W. Lawrence Hill was *in hell we crawl*, and Susie Isaacs was *sis is a U.S. ace*, and Lynne Loomis was *lemony loins*, and June Field and Phil Field were *if June led* and *he flip lid*, respectively. I myself was, and remain, *Josh van Hour*, as handsome a name as any Vorhaus-born could ever hope to have.

I further discovered that the Normandie Club was *manicure blond*, and the World Series of Poker was *flower spikers' rodeo*, and a royal flush was *a rush folly*, and three of a kind was *no fake dither*, and *Card Player* itself was *rarely patched* or *partly reached*. By then I felt I had opened a whole Pandora's box, or *darn soapbox*, so I put my anagram generator away for another day.

But the poker world has changed with the passing years. We now have Internet poker, an *entrée porn kit,* and poker cruises, *purse rockies,* and even new magazines such as *Poker Digest—top edge risk.* Herewith, then, more anagram madness, or *drama name snags,* as the case may be.

Among today's top players, we learn that Chris Ferguson is *four ring chess.* Annie Duke is *a nude Nike.* Melissa Hayden *dims an eyelash.* Mike Sexton is *next I smoke.* Barbara Enright is *Rabbit? Ha! Ranger!* Huck Seed? *He deck us.* Ken Flaton is *an elf knot.* Eskimo Clark says *risk me a lock.* Allen Cunningham? *He all cunning, man.*

Today's poker literati include Andy Glazer (*Dylan gazer*), Matt Lessinger (*mister tangles*), Barry Shulman (*blurry shaman*), Lou Krieger (*I, ego lurker*) and Greg Dinkin, otherwise known as the *eking grind.*

Do you like to visit the clubs and casinos? Perhaps you should know that Fort McDowell is *dwell comfort.* Hollywood Park is *OK, lord, how play?* Peppermill Casino is *a sim-*

ple con ripple. Ocean's Eleven is *one even scale*. At the Hustler Casino, *he turns social*. Crystal Park is *try racks, pal*.

Among Internet gaming sites, we find that pokerspot. com met *pro cop's okay*, while Paradise Poker is a *parkside opera*, Highlands Club has *chill bug hands,* poker.com is a *rock poem* and pokerpages.com is *mop or keg space*.

Out on the tournament trail, the Queen of Hearts is *a frequent hose*, while at the Queen of Diamonds *no foe mined quads*. The Winnin' o' the Green is a *renewing neon hit*, while the Orleans Open is a *noon relapse*, and at the World Poker Open *they do elk proper now*. A tournament itself is *one nut mart*. What are you gonna do?

You could play Omaha eight (*I'm a hate hog*) or crazy pineapple (*lazy pecan piper*) or Texas hold'em (*almost hexed*) or seven-card stud (*dusted caverns*) or even lowball (*blow all*). You could draw to an inside straight (*a hint: resist, dig?*). You could consider your implied odds (*I'd dip seldom*) and your win rate (*wit earn*) or expected value (*exclude tap eve*). Just don't forget to toke the dealer (*leaked thereto*) when you win.

More casinos: Sam's Town *owns mats*. At the Palace Station, *ace paints a lot*. The Golden Nugget *got gun legend*. At the Stratosphere, *hopes restart*. The Mirage says, *I'm gear* and at the Riviera *I arrive*. The Tropicana is *a coin trap*, but aren't they all? Including New York, New York, where *okay, Kenny, we worry*.

I could go on, you know. I could go on all night. That's the trouble with anagrams. Once you get started—*dart set*—it's hard to hit the brakes—*take his herbs*. Once you discover that a rebuy tournament is *me buoyant return*, you just won't be satisfied until you learn that the Book of Tells *be lots o' folk* too. After that, it all gets a little silly—*ill seal tilty*—and it's time to put the anagram generator away once more.

Ligara

There's always the question of what to do when someone lays a bad beat story—*toady barb set* (oh stop)—on us. When it happens to me, I give 'em a Bad Beat Receipt. If you clip and copy the following, you can do the same.

BAD BEAT RECEIPT c.jv.200X

LIGARA!

LIKE I GIVE A RAT'S ASS

DATE _____   SIGN HERE _____

Depends

There's also always the question of what to do when someone asks us for advice. I have a—necessarily equivocal—comeback for that as well.

The trouble with giving specific advice on specific situations is that you can never know enough, really, about the situation, to know if your advice is sound. You can be authoritative, well reasoned, and totally wrong. The trouble with asking for such advice is that it puts responsibility for your decision making on someone else's shoulders. You were there. You made the choice. Now analyze it, inspect it, evaluate it, then live with it; learn, and move on.

In poker, as in life, it's easy to second-guess yourself. In poker, as in life, it's easy to abdicate responsibility for the choices you make. Maybe someone else would have played your hand differently. Maybe the experts agree that you blundered. Who cares? Do you think you blundered? If yes, modify your play; if no, stick to your guns. What could be simpler than that?

Here, then, is my blanket response to those who would seek to know, for 100 percent sure, whether they made the right move at the right time or not. The answer is always . . .

It Depends

Poker is a challenge built on tendencies and trends
and many tough decisions upon which a session bends,
so when I'm asked for my advice by strangers or by friends,
I look them squarely in the eye and answer, "It depends."

Depends on who's been running hot,
who's on tilt and who is not,
how much money's in the pot,
and other things that I forgot.

Should you raise in late position?
Will that raise the blinds' suspicion?
I can take no firm position.
I am not a card magician
blessed with psychic precognition,
so I have no ammunition
for your poker combat mission.
I am just a politician
who, waffling, contends,
"It's poker, folks; it just depends."

Depends on who's been talking trash,
who has lots and lots of cash,
who's been drinking sour mash
(or maybe even smoking hash).

You want to know if you should bet a straight that half
    extends,

or push a pair of kings when on the flop an ace descends.
But if you ask me what a man of my keen judgment
   recommends,
I'll look you squarely in the eye and answer, "It depends."

Depends on who's a clever git,
or with the deck's been getting hit,
or who'll play any piece of—
(Don't use that word; it offends.
Let's just say it all depends.)

A check-raise on the turn, you want to know what that
   portends.
Is the raiser's raise legit or could it be he just pretends?
You wait for my reply, and how your disbelief suspends.
I'll look you squarely in the eye and answer, "It depends."

So if you want some confirmation
that your recent devastation
was just normal fluctuation,
(not some self-induced damnation)
I can feel your consternation,
but I fight against temptation
to provide you with salvation.
Though I want your admiration
I will risk disapprobation,
for I can't give affirmation
to your certain situation
without better information,
followed by some cogitation
and some subtle calculation
not to mention computation
to the point of constipation.

And now with no more hesitation
I'll complete your education

and leave you with this explanation:
Though the argument distends,
in the end, it all depends.

Thus reality transcends:
In the end it all depends.

Gamnesia

There's a game played among some smug intellectuals
where you add, subtract, or change one letter of an existing
word with an eye toward creating a whole new word with a
whole new meaning. Examples include *glibido,* all talk and
no action, and *osteopornosis,* a degenerate disease. This game
is, of course, a *divertissement* for people with far too much
time on their hands, plus the inflated sense of self-importance
that comes from knowing what words like *divertissement*
mean.

Being a person with far too much time on his hands, I
now offer these additions, subtractions, and alterations of the
poker lexicon (or *flexicon,* as it were; a more liberal dictionary):

Gamnesia. A bettor's tendency, strangely, to forget how
much money he lost.
Cashino. The place you go to lose yours.
Omahad. What you feel you've been when the river coun-
terfeits your low in Omaha/8.
Sournament. The state of mind you fall into when you
bust out on the bubble.
On the babble. The mindless, pointless stories you tell
about busting out on the bubble.
Fucktuation. It's easy to get mad when luck goes against
you, but please keep profanity to a minimum.

Hellmouth. What we call you when you keep profanity to a maximum.

Gutshop. To pay good money for a bad draw.

Statisick. How you feel when you look at your records and realize how bad you've been running.

Sadellite. The way you feel when you fail to money in the prelims.

Bottom pain. What you get if you go too far with bottom pair.

Cardshirk. He who makes no effort to improve his play.

C-not. What you have left when your last hundred is gone.

Dreck change. Don't bother asking; it won't even help.

Craparound. A big straight draw that doesn't get there.

Sueted connectors. When your premium draw turns into pig parts.

SETI-bluff. The search for intelligent life in your play.

Tap Mahal. A place to go broke in Atlantic City.

Follywood Park. A place to go broke in L.A.

Pocket aches. The brutal pain of one hand snapping.

Bell Hardens. And Commerce gets tougher too.

The rape. The rake.

Drawing deaf. When you ignore that little voice inside you telling you to fold.

Runner-ruiner. When you get one card you need, but not the next one.

World Series of Poke. A porn film you might have missed.

TOKES

A toke, as we know, is a tip: something you give to a dealer or waiter or your letter carrier at Christmastime. A tip can also be good advice or insider information. So then what follows are a few quick tokes, or tips, for energizing your poker game through some surprising—some might even say offbeat—strategies. You may think of these tokes as exercises or diversions or even just games. Their goal is to change, if only temporarily, the way you approach your play.

Tarot

There are so many different things to think about when we play poker. We have our resolutions—*I'm going to attack the damn blinds*—and we have our warnings—*don't overplay that stupid K-Q again*—and we have our affirmations and mantras—*no one can beat me but me.* With all these information streams flowing through our heads, it's hard sometimes to figure out what to focus on. Poker, sure, but saying to yourself, "Focus on poker" is like telling an astronomer, "Focus on the night sky, willya?" Where, specifically, would you have that astronomer look?

For an answer, strange as this seems, you might turn to a Tarot deck. Before your next poker session, pull out a Tarot deck (you can download one from the Internet) and select a card at random. Let that card be your inspiration and guide for the session to come. Let it give you resolutions and warnings and affirmations about the poker work you're about to do. Let it, in other words, filter and organize your approach to the task at hand.

You might, for example, reach into your Tarot deck and pull out the Page of Pentacles. According to my desktop interpretation of the Tarot (also downloaded from the Internet) the Page of Pentacles is careful and diligent, with respect for learning, scholarship, and new ideas. You might extract the meaning of this card thus:

> Today, when I go to play poker, I shall play with care and concentration, but keep an eye peeled for ways to turn recent learning into new targets of opportunity.

Does this sound hokey? Fine, let it sound hokey. Notice, though, how new information, even randomly acquired information, can give you a whole different perspective on your play.

Of course, you don't have to use the Tarot deck to acquire random information. You could read tea leaves or throw the I Ching. Hell, you can pull down any book from your bookshelf and read any arbitrarily selected sentence. This is from Robert A. Heinlein's *Time Enough for Love* (New York: Ace Books, 1974):

> Democracy is based on the assumption that a million men are smarter than one man.

How would you use this assertion to inform your poker? Just think about all the times you have been chided at the table for what your opponents perceived as bad play, or refused to chop a blind or make a final table tournament deal. You knew what you were doing, and you knew you were correct to do so, but their misguided peer pressure may have made you feel bad about yourself. Don't let tiny-minded majoricrats push you off an approach you know to be sound.

Now look what happens if you draw your random information from not just a book but a poker book. I open my dog-eared copy of *The Pro Poker Playbook* and I read the following words:

> As with Freemasonry, there are many degrees of poker consciousness. Someone who can instantly calculate pot odds versus card odds obviously has poker consciousness. Someone who consistently draws for a fifth king obviously does not. In between is the vast gray area inhabited by most of us.

This not-so-random bit of information serves to remind us that we're all on the road to somewhere. We're all trying to close the gap between where we are as poker players and where we desire to be. We are, in other words, in the vast gray area. If you keep this vast gray area in mind when you go to play poker today, you are likely to have confidence and yet humility about your own play, and you are also likely not to overestimate (and thus inappropriately fear) the power of your opponents.

You don't need the Tarot, tea leaves, or random reading in order to give yourself this sort of new information, but you do need *new information,* because it's entirely common to become stale in your poker thinking. Use devices such as the Tarot (or anything else you can think of) to keep your thinking fresh.

Silence

Here's a fun little game that's easy to play at the poker table: Just be silent. From the moment you walk into the card room until the moment you leave, pretend that you've lost the power of speech. You'll find that not talking has a very interesting impact on your game. For one thing, it focuses your attention by eliminating the distraction of conversation. For another thing, it cloaks you in a veil of mystery. Most of your opponents won't notice that you *don't say a word,* but they will notice that they're not getting a lot of chatter from your seat at the table. This will make you seem to be disciplined—perhaps more disciplined than you actually are. You will seem to be concentrating so fiercely on your poker that nary a word escapes your lips. This is a good thing.

There's more. Obviously if you're not talking, you're not telling bad beat stories, justifying loose calls, giving lessons at the table, or following any other counterproductive lines of yack. Whatever verbal tells you may have given away before, you won't give them away now. I know a guy (and I'm sure you do too, for every club has one) who stridently yells, "Pair the board!" when the last thing he wants is for the board to pair. I don't know if he thinks he's using reverse tells on his opponents or reverse psychology on the poker gods, but either way his words betray him every time he opens his mouth. If he kept his mouth shut, this wouldn't happen.

Also, in keeping silent, you are turning off your transmitter. This gives you more energy to devote to your receivers—your eyes and ears. In your silence, you will find that you concentrate on your opponents more easily and effectively, and extract much more useful information from their play. Your silence will also set you apart in your own mind. You will be *at* the table, but not *of* the table. This will help keep you centered in your game.

Your silence will require more precise actions. Since you won't be saying "raise" or "reraise" you'll have to make sure that your bets are full and complete when they leave your hand. By not announcing your raise, also, you become a quiet force at the table. People will have to reckon with you, because your raises just seem to *sneak in there* somehow.

Obviously you'll never ask for a deck change. Obviously you'll never criticize a lesser foe. Obviously you'll never whine or snivel. Or boast. Or rant. Or curse.

Silence is golden, they say. Try some on for size and see how much gold it can bring into your game.

Blackjack Attack

This toke has to do with your starting requirements, and the fact that, try as you might to stay tight, you inevitably let looseness slip into your game. For your next hold'em session, adopt the hard-and-fast rule that you will play *no hand* under *any circumstance* that's not a big pair or a natural blackjack 20 or 21. This gives you the following hands and no more: A-A, K-K, Q-Q, J-J, T-T, A-K, A-Q, A-J, A-T, K-Q, K-J, K-T, Q-J, Q-T, J-T. Further, for the sake of maintaining your discipline, tell yourself that if you play *any hand* other than *these hands,* you must get up from the table and leave the club immediately. This will have the effect of cementing your discipline to your desire. After all, you came to play, right? Playing so tight a regimen as the Blackjack Attack thwarts your desire to play many hands; however, if you tell yourself that broken discipline will result in *not getting to play at all,* then you'll give yourself the strength you need to be patient.

The Blackjack Attack makes it simple for you to tighten up your play because there's no ambiguity about whether a hand qualifies as a starting hand or not. It either is or it ain't. This will make it easier for you to achieve the goal of limiting the hands you play. When you achieve that goal, you'll derive the benefit of having done what you set out to do. This is no small thing, considering that so many of the external outcomes of poker (money lost or won) depend not on doing the right thing but on catching the right card. This way, win or lose, you can feel like a winner—a winner of discipline—when you walk away.

Call Waiting

Do you call too much and raise too rarely? Many people do. For those players I recommend the following toke: Tell yourself that for the next half hour or hour of play, calling is not an option. You can only raise or fold. The thinking behind this toke is that if your hand is worth a call, it's worth a raise.

We know of many situations in which, strategically, this is not true, but for the sake of this exercise, act as if it were. By eliminating "call" from your poker vocabulary, you will force yourself to consider more carefully whether you want to participate in the hand or not.

Obviously you will acquire an aggressive image, and couldn't you stand to have that? You may even acquire a maniac's image, and that wouldn't be a bad thing for you to experience either. Plus, look at it this way: If you never *just call,* you'll never make a loose call. If you never *just call,* you'll never make a crying call. If you never *just call,* you'll never be calling "just to keep them honest" or "for the size of the pot." Let the other guy engage in that nonsense!

Could a change like this fill some holes in your game? If not, then you're already raising appropriately and that's great; you don't need this strategy. But if *calling too much* is a disease you carry, then the *call waiting* toke may be just the cure for you.

Boistrosity

We've talked about playing a whole session in silence. Now let's contemplate the opposite of that. Win or lose, set your goal for your next session to be *the noisiest player at the table.* If you're a naturally timid person, you may find this hard to do. Once you get used to turning up the volume on your chat, however, you'll be amazed at some of the benefits you reap.

For one thing, big noise at the table always draws attention. Any attention your opponents pay to you, as we have already determined, is a little less attention that they pay to themselves. You may find that being a big talker also earns your bets a little more respect. The mere act of talking a lot suggests confidence, and people tend to give confident players a wide berth. This is especially useful if you don't *feel* particularly confident going into the game. Sure you're timid—maybe even you're scared—but *they* don't need to know that.

If you don't think that boistrosity is an image that fits you, just think about all the times that *that one loudmouth* at the table just seems to run over the game. You may not enjoy being *that one loudmouth,* but you'll certainly enjoy running all over the game.

Double Happiness

The next time you buy into your typical game, don't buy in for your typical amount. Instead, buy in for *double* that amount. You'll be amazed at how having twice as much money on the table allows you to be more aggressive and more fearless. Think about it: In most typical low- to mid-limit games, most players buy in for the convenient amount of one rack. That's, for example, $200 in a $6–$12 game. What happens, though, when you lose a stack or a stack and a half, and suddenly you're worried about having to buy more chips? If you already have a second rack, you've got sufficient bullets in your gun, and this problem goes away. Don't forget also that anyone who joins the game after you will naturally assume that you bought in for the typical amount, and thus are beating the game.

A perfect time to use this strategy is when a new game is just being spread. Let's say it's a $10–$20 game, and everyone is buying in for $500 or less. If you buy in for $1,000, you send a message to the table—*watch out, everyone, I'm loaded for bear!* Again, to anyone arriving after you, you look like the table's big winner.

If you're not comfortable putting a grand into a poker game, find a smaller game where you do feel comfortable purchasing that second rack. Try it. I think you'll like the difference it makes to your own thinking and your enemies', too.

> *Can you think of some tokes of your own? What little tricks or tips do you give yourself to put yourself or keep yourself on your game?*

GRABS

A "grab" is a poker concept you can grasp without much effort. Ever since I started playing poker, I have used grabs to focus my poker thinking. They're easy to understand and easy to recall, and they come in handy in many poker situations. I've listed some of my favorite grabs here for you, with appropriate commentary. I hope you find them useful—though I suspect you'll find your own grabs more useful still. Advice from outside sources is fine, but the advice you give yourself, in your own voice, will resonate much more strongly and harmoniously for you. So create a "grabs" section in your notebook and start saving all the succinct and clear-eyed observations you make while you play.

In the meantime, if you're looking for some compact ideas to chew on at odd moments, you might have a nosh on these:

> *Mixing up your play doesn't mean playing the same hands different ways, it means playing different hands the same way.*

Since it's almost always wrong to slow play a big pair into a big field, for example, you need to raise with big tickets whenever you can; you don't want to vary that play. If you don't vary something, however, then your attentive opponents will put you on the big hand you have. So you mix up your play by playing other hands exactly as you would your monsters. When you can make your 8-7 raise look just like your A-A raise, you've got half the field leaning the wrong way.

Go against the grain.

Conventional wisdom is for conventional thinkers. The best poker players have the ability to think creatively and originally about poker and poker situations. While the drones and clones are keeping close to the book (even this book) don't be afraid to write your own book. If you think you have a better idea, feel free to go against the grain. If nothing else, the unconventional nature of your play, as refracted through your thinking, will put your conventional opponents off-stride.

If it's good for a call, it's good for a raise.

Every time you say, "call" before the flop, you're saying that you think (or hope) that your hand will eventually be good enough to win. If you truly feel that way, why wouldn't you want more money in the pot? Of course, there are times when you'd rather encourage callers for the sake of building a volume pot with correct pot odds for your call, but in general we call too often and raise too rarely. The thinking behind *If it's good for a call, it's good for a raise* is not to get you to loosen up, but rather to strengthen up, and play your large hands in a large manner.

The long run is now.

How long is the long run? A month? A year? A lifetime? Who cares! Forget about the long run—how are you playing right now? Or look at it this way: No matter how long the long run is, today's action is part of it. If you're not doing your best *right now*, you can't expect to do your best over time.

> **Make the latest possible decision based on the best available information.**

Suppose you read your opponent's raise for an A-K and the flop comes little-little-little. If he keeps betting, do you put him on a bluff with overcards, or do you adjust and contemplate the possibility that he's pushing a big pair and was doing so all along? Smart players adjust continually throughout the hand, factoring in all actions, past and present, in order to form a coherent picture of their opponents' holdings. Make assumptions—but don't get married to them.

> **Only victims get victimized.**

People think it's bad luck when their two pair get pummeled by a higher two pair. Let's be frank: If you're in there with a low two pair in the first place, you're extremely vulnerable, and you should know it. Occasionally we're victimized by our opponents' superior play. Much more typically we're victimized by our own delusions, or wishful thinking, or loose calls with weak hands, or other victim-like behavior. We want to blame our opponents, but most of the time we have no one to blame but ourselves.

> **Each of us is responsible for his own good time.**

If you're in a crappy mood when you come to play poker, you can expect to play crappy poker. If you're lively and energetic, alive in the moment, and ready to bring your best game to this hand and every hand, you can expect to do much better. Poker is about math, sure, but it's also about mood. Make sure that yours is conducive to good play.

> *Don't beat your head against a wall that has a door in it.*

Sometimes the simplest solution is the best. If your opponent's raise seems to represent a hand, and you have no reason to believe he's bluffing, by all means credit him for the hand he has! Fold, and move on. How much punishment do you need to take, especially in poker, where punishment equals poverty? Absent hard evidence to the contrary, the easy thing and the sensible thing is usually the right thing too.

> *If you're not steadily getting better, you're steadily getting worse.*

Yesterday's tactics don't work in today's game. If your opponents know what they're doing, they're already hard at work adjusting to your play. If they don't know what they're doing—God love them—you stand to maximize your advantage by constantly improving your own play. Get relentlessly better. Don't let the whole world (or anyway, the poker world) pass you by.

> *It doesn't matter whether you're in the front or the back of a bus that's going over a cliff.*

We often delude ourselves in poker, seeking reasons for optimism when, frankly, pessimism is called for. If you're beaten, you're beaten. Don't allow yourself to believe that a couple of lucky cards and a couple of tricky plays will turn you into a vastly superior opponent against vastly superior opponents. Cut your losses while you still have the chance. Get off the bus before it goes over that cliff.

> *A lie is not a lie if the truth is not expected.*

Don't neglect the opportunity to bet when it's clear that the first bet wins. There are frequent situations in which people can't call, even if they know you're a lying sack of cheese. This is called "the right of first bluff," and if you don't exercise the right when you have the chance, you're turning your back on free money.

The other side is always evil.

In any battle for survival, moral justification is an integral weapon of the war. Morality, it has been said, is just the tool that both sides use to validate unspeakable horrors committed in the name of survival. The same is true in poker. Your enemies seem evil because they're out to get you. Guess what? You seem evil too, because you're out to get them. Never underestimate the strength you enjoy simply by being in opposition.

The universe is there to sort you out.

Nobody cares about your bad beats, and you shouldn't either. You should only care about what your bad beats teach you. Do they make you stronger? Do they improve your play, your steely resolve, and your mind-set? Bad beats are inevitable, and besides: *There are no bad beats, only temporary setbacks.* Treat them as the learning experiences they are.

Blessed are the weak, for they shall inherit the flop.

Weak players love cheap flops. They don't want to raise, and they don't want you to raise. They don't want anything interfering with the fun they get out of seeing that flop. Deny them that fun. If you have a hand that warrants a raise, then raise. Punish them for their atavistic urges—not because you hate them, but just because you love their money.

Save your ego for the winner's circle.

Poker should be about cards and chips and winning. Too often it becomes a dick-measuring contest. When your ego gets involved—when your desire to prove your superiority becomes the guiding light of your game—you are lost. Save your ego for the winner's circle. After you've proven how good you are, then you get to boast.

If you can't be right, be loud.

Announce your bets and raises—and even your folds and checks—in a loud, self-assured voice. Do this for two reasons: First, if you announce all your actions with confidence, you will ultimately acquire confidence as well. This is the Buddhist concept of *right action, right mind*: Take the action you wish to take, in the way you wish to take it, and your mind will eventually come along for the ride. Second, if you announce all your actions in the same forceful tone, you'll make it more difficult for your foes to find tells in your inconsistencies.

Don't bite the hand that feeds your bankroll.

If you're beating up on some weakie, and he's giving you all his money, don't do anything—*anything*—to distract him from his task. Especially don't berate him when he draws out on you. He has to draw out on you every once in a while in order to maintain his enthusiasm for the game, and for the job of feeding your bankroll. Nurture the weakies. As the saying goes, "Don't tap on the glass."

It's not the end of the world; it's not even the end of the week.

Poker offers you a shot at redemption on the very next hand. Put your losses behind you. The only thing that matters on this hand is *this hand*.

> *Money is only important to people who don't
> have anything important in their lives.*

Does poker rule your life? Or does it exist in the context of a conscious, well-balanced, self-aware existence? It may surprise you to learn that the less obsessive you are about your poker, the better your game might be. Why? Because if poker is all you have going on in your life—if *getting that money* is the only thing that matters to you—you'll be so hooked on outcome, and so dependent on a positive outcome, that the pressure of performance will cripple you. Vary your interests. Live a full life. Then your poker can be the triumphant experience you want it to be—in its proper place.

> *If you look harder, you'll see better.*

Look harder in all directions: Study your poker texts; study your opponents; but most of all, *study yourself.* Do you, for example, play "getaway hands"? Do you loosen up your starting requirements when you're about to leave the game, just in the hope of winning that last, lucky pot? More often than not, you end up giving back part of your win—sometimes all of it. This wouldn't happen if you knew, really knew, that you were at risk for getaway hands. Know yourself—just know yourself—everything follows from that.

> *State the five most important things you know
> about poker in the simplest possible way.*

FAQ

Nobody asks questions like poker players ask questions. "Should I raise with J-T suited in late position?" "Should I stay in a good game even if I'm losing?" "Why is the coffee here so bad?" Sometimes the answers are so self-evident that we wonder why anybody bothers to ask. Sometimes the answer is that old poker standby, "It depends." Sometimes the questions are asked so frequently that they earn the title *frequently asked questions,* or FAQ. Here are a few FAQ that I've been asked or, you know, made up.

Should I wear headphones at the table?

If you're wearing headphones to drown out the distraction of other players, especially the ones who are trying to put you on tilt with their talk, then by all means wear headphones. Recognize, however, that when you put on those 'phones, you're cutting yourself off from audio input. Players say a lot of things they don't know they're saying. If the guy to your left mutters, "Stupid kings," as he mucks his hand after an ace hits the board, you'll know he can be moved off his big pairs. That's information you'd like to have, and the sort of audio cue you might miss if you have the Beatles cranked up on your CD player.

Some people listen to music to relax their minds while they play. If that's you, that's fine, but if you listen to music (or sports or Spanish Made E-Z) because you're just not sufficiently stimulated by the poker you're playing and you need another information stream to keep your mind occupied, then I'd say you have a problem. Focus on the game! If poker by itself is not enough to keep your busy mind from getting bored then you're not doing it right.

What about sunglasses? Is it useful to hide my eyes?

Again, if the strategy gives you more than it costs you, that's fine. While it's absolutely true that dark or mirrored sunglasses will keep your opponents from gaining any tells from your eyes, those same glasses may cut down on the amount of useful visual information you receive. Suppose you have trouble distinguishing suits because of your dark glasses. This may cause you to peek at your hole cards a little longer, or hold those cards a little higher, giving prying eyes an extra chance to pry in on you. Those glasses are there to protect you. Make sure they're not having the opposite effect.

Some players favor dark glasses and headphones for the mysterioso image these accessories project. You give the impression of being alone in your own little citadel of poker, impervious and unassailable. Does your play reflect this reality? Then your image is serving you. I prefer the flexible alternative of a cap with a bill. When the situation calls for inscrutability, I can pull the hat down low over my eyes. When I'd rather present myself as friendly and accessible—an image I can often use to my advantage—then I tilt my cap back and expose my smiling face.

How much money do I need to buy in at a given limit?

At minimum, you should be prepared to put as much money on the table as the average stack size at that table when you sit down to play. In most games, one rack of chips is considered the standard: one hundred $1 chips at $3–$6, two hundred $2 chips at $6–$12, and so on. You never want to buy in for significantly less than the table average, because you always run the risk of being attacked if you're perceived to be outgunned.

Remember, though, if you don't feel comfortable buying into a game for the table average, buying in short is not the answer. Rather, go find a smaller game, where your buy-in will go that much further and seem that much bigger, relative to the size of the game.

How big of a bankroll do I need for, say, $20–$40?

Well, let's see. If you plan to play $20–$40 only once in your life and then never again, you don't need a bankroll any bigger than your buy-in. If, however, you intend to compete regularly at that level, you need enough cash behind you to withstand the inevitable bankroll fluctuations you'll face. Some players use a rule of thumb called "ten times to the well." They want their bankroll to be at least ten times the size of their typical buy-in, figuring that they could then endure ten consecutive rack-offs before going broke.

People run bad; it's a fact. There's no shame in gearing down if your bankroll is imperiled. Should you reach the point where a couple of bad sessions at your typical limit could put you out of action at that limit, just slide down a level or two and build your bankroll back up. For instance, if you've been playing $10–$20 with a $5,000 bankroll, and you get down to around two grand, go find a $6–$12 game where your remaining $2,000 will cover you again to the tune of ten buy-ins.

In all events, don't play in a big game with a small bankroll because short money is scared money: You'll play afraid, and therefore won't play your best.

What does it mean to "slide left"?

Some players have a practice, when a seat opens to their left, of routinely moving into that seat, a practice they call "sliding left." Their thinking is that the next player into the game will be an unknown quantity, and they'd rather have the advantage of position over that unknown quantity while figuring out his play. Chances are he won't be significantly better than anyone already at the table, but if he were, the last thing one would want is to yield a favorable position to such a player.

Any time you change seats, of course, there's a certain amount of trade-off. In sliding left, you may be giving up position on a player you already dominate, or moving further out of position against another dominating player. All other things being equal, though, you might as well slide left and put "the devil you don't know" on your right.

When should I turn pro?

Probably never. The difference between making a living playing poker and supplementing your income with poker is just vast and huge. It's not that there's *not* money to be made in the game; there is. However, when you're relying on poker to make your monthly nut, it changes your approach to the game. It increases your sense of urgency and decreases your joie de vivre, both of which changes can lead to negative outcomes.

With some notable exceptions, those who do best with their poker are those who play winning poker in the context of other winning endeavors. They get the best of both worlds: the extra income that successful poker play can bring, without the debilitating financial insecurity that full-time pros must face.

Plus—without waxing too philosophical here—if you're playing poker for a living, all you're really doing is moving money around a table and trying to move most of it off the table and into your pocket. You're not making anything, building anything, or helping the world in any material sense. Of course, it's up to you to decide what you want to do with your life, but do you really want your sole legacy to be *he played some excellent poker?* Great as that is, to me it's not enough.

SUMMARY

Let's have a look back at some of the key concepts in this book. You may find it easier to refer to them here than to dig them out of the text.

Loose call bad, loose raise good.

If you're going to play loose, drive *loose. When you're betting, you're in command. Let your foes be the ones to make the bad loose calls.*

Go big or go home.

If you can't be bold at the poker table, you have no hope of winning. The cautious, timid, and careful may survive, but only the strong can thrive.

When you get the goods, bet the goods.

Too often, we're too tricky. Thinking we have a monster, we decide to slow play, only to discover that we've inadvertently allowed an inferior hand catch up. Conversely, convinced that our table image is bulletproof, we bluff with vastly inferior cards. When you get the goods, bet the goods. When you don't have the goods, *don't bet.* Do *just this one thing* right, and you'll be able to beat most of the games most of the time.

Short money equals lost money.

If you buy into a poker game for substantially less than the table average, you will be overrun and destroyed. If you don't feel comfortable buying in for at least the table average, find a smaller game.

You're born broke, you die broke; everything else is just fluctuation.

So don't sweat it. Really. You don't need to be so upset. The more upset you are, the more negative fluctuation you'll have, not just in terms of money but also in terms of tranquility and peace of mind. It seems like a paradox, but it's not: The less you care about the money, the more you're likely to win.

> *The only one who can beat you is you.*

Remember, you're there to punish other players, not yourself. You're not nearly so much at risk from others' superior play as you are from flaws in your own approach. Think about it: Other opponents are involved against you only occasionally, but *you're involved* in every hand you play. If you play badly, it doesn't matter whether they play well or not—you can't expect to win.

> *To read other people's minds, start by reading your own.*

Everyone thinks pretty much the same thoughts. If you're honest about yours, you can reliably predict theirs. Also, see yourself as others see you. If they think you're tricky, you can play honestly and win; if they think you're straightforward, you're granted a license to steal.

> *Self-indulgence = self-destruction.*

If you're doing things at the poker table just to feel better about yourself, chances are the strategy will backfire and you'll end up feeling worse. Make wise choices and allow yourself to feel good about positive outcomes, not negative urges.

> *Don't challenge strong players, challenge weak ones; that's what they're there for.*

You can't make most of your money against players who know better, so your first job should be to locate, engage, and attack the ones who don't. To win at poker, you don't have to be a great player or even a good one, just better than the bad ones.

Afterword

You know, when I started this book, I thought it was going to be Killer Poker this and Killer Poker that. I envisioned Killer Poker hats, shirts, coffee mugs, pins, spinners, and chips. Now, as I finish writing, I think that Killer Poker is a fine point of departure, but it's certainly not the defining thought of expert poker play, nor even, as it turns out, the defining thought of this book.

Certainly it pays to be aggressive; certainly most of us could stand to be more aggressive than we naturally are; and certainly a controlling idea like *"Raise!"* for example, can serve to remind us where, when, and how to activate the aggressiveness within. Aggressiveness without thoughtfulness, however, is just the spinning of so many wheels. So if I had to come up with a two-word phrase that captures the essence of this book, it would not be Killer Poker. No, here's what it would be:

Be honest.

Be honest with yourself about your reasons for playing. Be honest about your skill level. Be honest about your flaws. Be honest about your strengths. Be honest about your chances of making poker your career, or even your net-plus avocation. Be honest about the positive and negative effects that an obsession with poker can have upon your life. Be honest with your non-poker-playing loved ones. Be honest in your dealings with others (beat them soundly—but fair and square!). Be honest with your records. Be honest about your state of mind. Be honest. That's all. That's what Killer Poker is really all about in the end.

Thank you for reading this book. I welcome your comments (jv@vorza.com) and look forward to our next poker voyage together.

Glossary
A Few Words on Words

In linguistic philosophy we learn that language informs belief: Manipulate language and you manipulate belief. All-knowing, all-seeing gods aren't all-anything to the true believers until someone labels them as such. The words *for a limited time only* can induce a spending frenzy among people who would otherwise not shop and not buy—but what has that to do with poker?

Poker, as we know, is about concentration. The better you concentrate, the better you play. What seems like a wildly self-indulgent exercise in naming things (this glossary) is really a means of focusing concentration. By naming things, and by referring to these things by name, we quickly move to a deeper level of understanding; we "know" these things better than we did before.

Suppose you describe a tight table as a *rock garden*. If this phrase is in your head, then when you see a tight game in progress and identify it by name, you suddenly have a higher awareness of that game, its strengths, weaknesses, pitfalls, and possibilities. It's a shorthand, sure, and not a foolproof one, but it gives you a point of reference. By titling the elements of the game, you know them better than you otherwise would.

Even more than understanding, there's *raw power* in words—especially private words and phrases that you alone know. God gave Adam and Eve the job of naming all the plants and animals and the worms in the dirt and the "fishies" in the sea. Then God gave them *dominion* over these things—ownership. Name a thing and you own it, too.

How is this useful in poker? Hey, how is it not? You're sitting in a mid-limit stud game, and you notice that one of the players routinely gets out ahead of his hand. You silently assign that player a name—you call him *rabbit*, because that's what they call a marathon runner who jumps out to an early lead, only to burn out and finish well back in the pack. Once you name this poker rabbit, he's *yours*. You know that his bets consistently mean less than they should, and this gives you an edge you can exploit.

Inventing and using new poker slang, then, will actually *make you a better player*. If you make it your business to name things in your game, you can't help but focus on the game you're in. Focus equals concentration, and concentration equals profit in poker. That's why I name things every chance I get.

Some people have challenged my right to do this. "JV," they've said, calling me by my own slang name for myself, "where the hell do you get off making up new words for things? What gives you the right to reinvent language to suit your whim?" Good question. One I've contemplated for many long days and nights before dismissing it altogether.

After all, we reinvent language all the time. Just think of the words and phrases we use daily that did not exist scant years ago: Ebola virus, computer virus, broadband, eBay, ATM, SUV, virtual reality, Omaha/8, Enron, shareware, outplacement, hyperspace, and so on.

The thing is, these words didn't come out of nowhere. Someone, somewhere, coined each of them, uttered every

last one for the very first time. Language is an act of creation, an *individual* act of creation. Everything that follows
is just adoption and adaptation and convention and con-
sensus.

This glossary, then, is my act of poker slang creation.
You can take or leave what you see fit. Choose the words
and phrases you like and claim them for your own. Or ignore them all. Either way is fine with me.

However, definitely do this: Invent your own slang. To
name a thing is to own a thing, and your own definitions
for your routine poker problems, opportunities, opponents,
or situations will inform you more deeply about your own
game than any words of mine. It's an exciting freedom, one
we don't routinely get from teachers or parents or peers,
but now you're getting it from me. You have my permission
to invent new words. Invent as many as you like, for any
situation whatsoever. Do it! Try it! It's fun, it makes you
alive in your mind, and it may even put a few more berks
in your bankroll.

Absolute Zero. When the cards are *that* cold.
Active Sonar. A raise made early to determine who has hidden
    strength. It's not a bad strategy to ping your opponents, but
    watch out if they ping you back!
ACV. Actual Cash Value. An honest bet based on legitimate
    strength. ACV players almost never bluff.
Anticoagulant. A good player who helps a bad player bleed lots
    and lots of money into the game.
ATM Cards. These are the kind of cards that cost you lots and lots
    of money. Non-nut lows or non-nut flushes in Omaha/8, for
    example. Everyone has their own special ATM cards. When
    you're tired, really, really tired, they're *all* ATM cards.
Balk. A type of angle shot where you hesitate before betting to see
    if people behind you intend to call, fold, or raise.
Bandana Bet. A raise made in late position with good cards. It
    looks as if you're out to steal the blinds, but you actually have

hidden power; so not only are you a robber, you're wearing a disguise.

Big Ben. A hundred-dollar bill.

Bigfoot. A high kicker: "We both had aces, but I got stomped by his bigfoot." Try not to play high cards without bigfoot to protect you.

Big Maxx and Baby Maxx. Hold'em hands: the king and queen of clubs, and queen and jack of clubs, respectively. Origin unknown.

Big Noise. The most active player at the table, the one everyone else defers to or respects or loathes and fears.

Birthday Card. The miracle card you really don't deserve, but get just the same. Well, hell, everyone has a birthday.

Blitzkrieg. A strategy for entering a game and playing superaggressively with the intention of taking over the game by intimidation alone.

Bluffalo. When you're not bluffing but they think you are, you've got 'em bluffaloed.

Bottom Feeder. A low-limit scrounge artist hoping to eke out small wins against weakies. Also someone who plays bottom pairs all the way to the river.

Bracelet Play. A clever or crafty move, the sort of play you'd make to win a World Series of Poker bracelet. It's generally useless in low-limit ring games.

Brickhouse. A losing full house.

Bump It or Dump It. Raise or fold. Not the worst strategy in the world, especially if you're trying to add an element of aggressiveness to your game.

Bus Driver. The person who controls the betting. Remember that only the bus driver knows for sure where the bus is going, so *grab the wheel.*

Calling Station. A loose-passive player who calls far more than he should.

Chair Glue. The stuff that keeps a stuck player stuck. It's not enough to know that it's time to quit; you also need the strength to overcome the inertia of sitting there. Don't let poverty be the thing that ultimately drives you from your seat.

Chastity Belt. A player's self-imposed loss limit designed to keep him from getting screwed. "Jane took off her chastity belt when she put her second Big Ben into the game."

Chip Remover. Any alcoholic beverage, so called because of the effect it has on your stack of chips. "Frank was doing fine till he started hitting the chip remover."

Chip Weevil. Someone who nibbles away at your stack.

Cinderella Catch. A miracle card on the river.

Clang or Clanger. A useless card named for the sound it makes when it hits your hand.

Coffin Catch. A card good enough to keep you in the hand, but not good enough to let you win.

Command Post. Seat held by the strongest player in the game. "I had the command post from the moment I sat down."

Company Town. A game filled with locals, where everyone knows everyone and nobody knows you.

Condom Bet. A raise made to protect the leading hand against drawing hands.

Containment Vessel. A player's discipline. Losing that discipline equals a crack in the containment vessel.

Copycat Crime. An attempt to steal the blinds two hands in a row.

Corking. Going on tilt. Not just going on tilt but actually turning into "a cork, bobbing on the sea of poker." All of us find ourselves in this hapless state of mind at one time or another. The trick is to get out of the water before you're swept out to sea and drowned.

Critical Mass. The number of bad beats a player must experience before he goes on tilt.

Dawn Patrol. Players in a game that lasts all night.

Day Care. A game filled with retirees.

Death Benefit. Money donated to complete an all-in player's incomplete bet.

Defenestrate. Literally "to throw out a window," in tournament terms it's the tendency of a losing player to toss away his last few chips on hopeless draws or bad hands.

Delivery Boy. A young or inexperienced player. "The delivery boy in seat six bet his bottom pairs all night."

Dilbert. Strong on math, weak on skills. "That Dilbert knows all the odds, but can't pull the trigger on a raise."

Dimmer Switch. Gradual growing weariness. When you start getting dimmer switched, it's time to turn off the lights and go home.

Double Infinity. A pair of eights.

Draft Dodger. Someone who changes seats or tables to avoid paying blinds or collection.

Drain Pipe. An unassuming player who slowly but steadily sucks your money away.

Duck Bucket. A pair of deuces, or any poor holding that holds up. When you lose to such a hand, you've been hit with the duck bucket.

Easter Egg Hunt. A loose, passive game where almost everyone plays almost every hand.

ECM. Electronic countermeasures, such as wearing headphones at the table to cut down on distraction.

Elvis. Someone with a perilously short stack who simply refuses to die. "Gretchen won the tournament; she was a total Elvis in the middle rounds."

Eyewash. Deceptive words or deeds. "You can't trust Tommy's tells. They're all eyewash."

Fingerprint. A player's signature move. "Albert always check-raises Big Maxx in early position. It's his fingerprint."

Firebug. A reckless raiser who puts the entire table, himself included, on tilt.

Fireproof. A strong, stable player who cannot be put on tilt. "The strength of Larry's game is he's totally fireproof."

Fish and Chips. Lots of really bad players with lots of loose cash.

Flag Football. A friendly little game where no one raises and no one really gets hurt.

Flame Out. In tournament play, to squander a big chip lead and bust out in the course of a few hands.

Flip-Flop. A flop that makes your good hand bad, like J-J-T in Omaha/8 when you hold A-2-3-4.

Flock. Of sheep or pigeons. A table full of weak players.

Floorman. An alternative expletive. Say this instead of that other f-word, and you won't risk the penalties that some tournaments impose for bad language. As in, "That floormanning dealer always deals me such floormanning bad cards. I was leading all the way but I got floormanned on the floormanning river. Motherfloormanner!"

Flop Fever. A disease spread by flopheads. Good when other players catch it, bad when you do.

Flophead. Someone who swears to see the flop, the whole flop, and nothing but the flop, so help him God.

Floptimist. Someone who believes that any two cards can win.

Food Stamps. Household budget pressed into bankroll duty. "Ol' Maurice is playing with his food stamps again."

Fool's Paradigm. The logic by which a losing player justifies his loss.

Foreclosure Raise. A check-raise made on the flop from an early position designed to induce a check (and possibly a free card) on the turn. If you flop an open-ended straight draw, for example, and make a foreclosure raise, then you can bet again if you hit your straight on the turn, or just check if you miss.

Franklin. To lose money by the hundreds. "I Franklin'd for about five hours last night."

Freight Train Through the Wind. An unstoppably good or hot player. "Tina went through that tournament like a freight train through the wind."

Fringe Benefits. Dead money in the pot. "Sam contributes a fringe benefit or two on almost every hand."

Gack. To fold winners. "Mirabelle had me outkicked, but she gacked when I raised."

Gamnesia. A bettor's tendency, strangely, to forget how much money he lost.

Gargle. To play a long session without winning or losing very much at all.

Getaway Hand. A hand you play when you're about to leave the table. Often one you wouldn't be caught dead playing normally—and probably shouldn't be caught dead playing now. To play strong, *finish* strong.

Get Well Card. A card that wins you a big pot and brings you back to even. Might be a good time to go home and finish convalescing.

Ghosting. Inhabiting the minds and thoughts of other players when you're not in the hand, and measuring their actions against what you would do in their situation. Ghosting is an effective way to hone your concentration, your observational skills, and your grasp of other people's play.

Gopher. An optimist. Someone who'll "go fer" any draw at all.

Graze. To limp in or flat-call with weak cards. "Frank was just graz-

ing in late position, but hit a straight draw and got trapped."
Cows graze. Sheep graze. Don't you graze too.

Hail Mary. To go all-in with a bad hand. "Terry went hail Mary
with 9-5 suited."

Handcuffed. Trapped by your own hand or your own bad play.
"Maggie bluff-raised before the flop, then got handcuffed
when the button reraised."

Hawkeye. Someone who tries to sneak peeks at other players'
cards.

Helium Atmosphere. A general tendency to raise. "It was a quiet
game until the helium atmosphere took over."

Hemorrhaging at the Wallet. Losing lots and lots of money very,
very fast.

Hit-to-Win. The sort of (usually low-limit) game where you mostly
need the best hand to take the pot. If everyone at the table is
playing hit-to-win, then you should bluff less often and bet for
value more.

Honeymoon. Your first few hands in a new game. You may be able
to steal a pot or two during your honeymoon because the
other players don't feel they have a line on you yet.

Hoover Bet. A small bet with a strong hand on an early street in
seven-card stud, designed to suck in players with weaker
hands.

House Arrest. In seven-card stud, when you make two pair on the
first four cards and don't improve from there.

Iceberg. Hidden power. "I put him on a pair of kings, but he had
an iceberg straight."

Imploder. Someone who needles another player in an effort to get
him or her to go on tilt.

Inside Out. An out card that fills an inside straight or some other
equally improbable dream. If you play inside out too much,
that's what your opponents will turn you.

Isotope. An unstable or volatile player, someone who's easily im-
ploded.

Jackthree. To get garbage holdings, like hold'em's J-3 offsuit. "I've
been nothing but jackthreed all night long."

Kingfisher. Someone who continues to play a pair of kings despite
an ace on the flop and multiple raises.

Komodo Dragon. A seemingly scary player who turns out not to
be as strong as he appears.

Labrador Retriever. Someone who goes broke, leaves the table to get more money, comes back to the game, and loses that money, too.

Liquid Wrench. Another name for booze. It has a tendency to loosen things up.

Little Foot. A small kicker.

McGruff. The crime dog. A person who always calls, "just to keep 'em honest."

Mental Muck. A tell by which some players betray, by their body language or eye movement, their intention to muck a hand. Look downstream for the mental muck before you make your move.

MIRV. Multiple Independently Targeted Re-entry Vehicle. A hand, especially an Omaha/8 hand, that has several different ways to win.

Noise Pollution. People who talk and talk and *talk* about nothing at all at a poker table. Sometimes it's done for image, and it can be devastating. Mostly it's just habit and reveals a compulsive yacker's mental weakness.

Nuthouse. The nut full house—and where you want to go when four of a kind beats it.

Okey-Tokey. A donation station, and a friendly, agreeable one at that.

Omaholics. The name given to fans of Omaha/8. Also known as *omacidal maniacs.*

On the Couch. Broke, out of action; home watching TV.

Orbit. Once around the table in a flop game. "I went three orbits before I found a hand I could play."

Over the Rainbow. Starting with a mixed-suit (rainbow) flop, you catch runner-runner for a flush. You found your hand over the rainbow.

Oxygen-Debt Stupidity. The thing that makes a tired player keep playing long after his brain has gone to bed.

Pisa. Leaning, like the tower—about to go on tilt.

Pocket Veto. The higher of two hidden pairs. "I had jacks wired but got pocket vetoed by his queens."

Pogo Stick. A volatile player who wins and loses a number of large pots in succession.

Power Shortage. When everyone "checks to the power," and the power checks too.

Preaching to Geese. Making tricky or sophisticated plays into players too dimwitted to appreciate them.

Premium Blend. A superior style of play. You confine yourself mostly to quality cards but mix up your play from time to time. It's premium blend play to take an inexpensive flier on a mid-level holding that's likely to be a strong hand if it hits.

Presbyterian Poker. An exceedingly polite and well-behaved game.

Program Bet. A betting scheme or sequence developed in advance and implemented under certain circumstances. Someone who plans to defend his blind against a blind stealer by check-calling any flop then check-raising any turn is employing a program bet.

Projectile Vomiting. Losing lots of money very fast and very painfully.

Psyops. Psychological operations. Another name for image play.

Pure Real Estate. A position bet. When you raise on the button with nuttin', that's pure real estate.

Pure Sinkhole. A position bet that backfires and costs a lot of money.

Putting Ben Gay in Their Shorts. Not just beating someone, but taunting them when you do.

Quick Lunch. A hand that's folded by everyone except the blind.

Rabbit. A player who gets out ahead of his hand.

Rack Off. To buy in for a rack and play through it quickly and poorly.

Rathole. To secretly remove chips from the table. Also a name for the house drop.

Rock Garden. A game in which most of the players are tight and timid. Not a great garden for growing stacks.

Rose Garden. A game in which most of the players are weak and loose. A much more fruitful flower bed.

Scavenger Hunt. The search for a weak, soft, beatable game.

Severance Pay. The odd chip that a disgusted player throws at the dealer when he busts out of a game.

Sham Dunk. A successful bluff.

Shoplift. To steal the blinds or antes. You can't be a successful poker player without a little shoplifting every now and then.

Shrapnel. Secondary devastation caused by a player going explosively on tilt and bringing a measure of bad play to everyone around him. "Brooks went broke, of course, but I caught a little shrapnel too."

Skinny. Information. Another name for a tell. "Jerome gives good skinny on his monsters."

Smokequarium. The glass-walled smoker's lounge in California card rooms.

Smokestack. Lots of chips in the hands of a weak player, because you know it's only time until that stack turns to smoke.

Speed-Tilt. The worst kind of tilt, it's triggered by a single mistake or a single bad beat. When the damage is done before you know what hit you, you've been hit by speed-tilt.

Sphinx. A strong, silent rock.

Splitsophrenics. Players addicted to high/low split games.

Stonewall. A tough rock; a player who's solid and strong. Best to go around a stonewall, rather than through.

Stupid Connectors. Low, unsuited connectors in hold'em

Surprise Party. A hand that shouldn't win, but does.

Switchboard. A turn card that changes the value of your hand. Similar to a flip-flop. "I was on a flush draw, till the switchboard gave me low trips."

Table Dance. To change tables for the sole purpose of presenting yourself (falsely) as a weak, scared player running away from a tough, unprofitable game.

Test Tube Baby. Someone new to card room poker, but with lots of experience in computer simulation games.

Thrift Shop. Penny-ante poker game.

Toll Road. A game with lots of pre-flop raising—it'll cost you plenty to drive here.

Tourniquet. A rebuy tournament that ends up costing you lots more than you ever intended to spend.

Triggerfish. A weak player who consistently leads the betting.

Trojan Horse. Hidden strength. "I flopped top pair, but Sandy's low set was a Trojan horse."

Tyrant. Someone whose reckless raises tend to control the action in a game.

U-Boat. In seven-card stud, a full boat with no pairs showing.

Umbilical. Someone who won't let go of a hand. "You can raise into Ed all day; he's an umbilical with an ace in his hand."

Vapor Lock. A brain condition that makes hands such as 9-2 suited seem playable.

Variety Store. A dealer's choice game.

Ventriloquist's Dummy. Someone who raises into another player when that other player already holds the nuts.

Victoria's Secret. A strong female player masquerading as a weak one.

Vitamin P. Your daily dose of poker.

Vultch. After "vulture." To feed on loose, tilted, or otherwise disabled players. "He's not much good against the big boys, but boy can he vultch the weakies."

Wally. Short for Cally Wally: a loose, passive player who can be counted on to call with inferior values and to raise only with superpremium hands.

Ways and Means. Powerful cards backed by the will to bet them. You can't win at poker without the ways and means.

Weakies. Timid players. Don't forget to eat your weakies.

Whisk Broom. A sweeper. Both halves of the pot in a split-pot game.

White Noise. Irrelevant table talk.

Wobble Raise. A raise made in an effort to isolate and test players suspected of being weak. With or without strong card values, you can make such a raise against such opponents, just to see if they'll wobble and fall over.

Wolf Pack. A bunch of locals who know each other well and specialize in carving up the tourists.

Woodentop. An ignorant blockhead, oak from the neck up.

Worsify. To degrade your opponents' capabilities through specific actions or image plays designed to make them leave optimum strategy behind and play worse than they otherwise would.

X-Ray Specs. An uncanny ability to read other players or anticipate their hands. "Delilah's wearing X-ray specs today."

Yellow Pages. A bet or an image play made strictly for advertising purposes, such as revealing a bluff after everyone has folded.

Yogi. Someone who insists on teaching other people how to play. Also known as swami or perfessor. "I wish this yogi would just shut up and let the delivery boy keep drawing dead."

Zeppelin. A player who's ponderous or slow to act.

Zero Hour. Quitting time in a home game. "Floris was hoping to get even before zero hour."

Zipper. A trap play. "I checked on the flop and check-raised on the turn. He was totally caught in the zipper."

Zloty. Low stakes. Named after the Polish coin. "It was a zloty game, but I still managed to win a hundred bucks."

Zombie. The undead. Someone who's stayed in the game all night or longer.

Resources

BOOKS

Though I could recommend many more books than room here allows, some that have helped me most include:

Brunson, Doyle: *Super/System: A Course in Power Poker*
Caro, Mike: *Caro's Fundamental Secrets of Poker*
Caro, Mike: *Mike Caro's Book of Tells: The Body Language of Poker*
Fox, John: *Play Poker, Quit Work and Sleep Till Noon*
Jones, Lee H: *Winning Low Limit Hold'em*
Krieger, Lou: *Hold'em Excellence: From Beginner to Winner*
Krieger, Lou: *More Hold'em Excellence: A Winner for Life*
McEvoy, Tom: *Tournament Poker*
McEvoy, Tom, and Cloutier, T. J: *Championship Hold'em*
Percy, George: *Seven-Card Stud: The Waiting Game*
Sklansky, David: *The Theory of Poker*
Yardley, Herbert O: *The Education of a Poker Player*

WEBSITES

Any list of websites will naturally become outdated over time, as sites change, merge, morph, or vanish into the vast abyss of *file not found*. As of this writing, some key sources of online poker information include:

rec.gambling.poker: The definitive discussion group for poker pros and aficionados, it can be accessed through www.groups.google.com

www.cardplayer.com: This site offers archived content from the magazine as well as general gaming information and an online poker bookstore.

www.conjelco.com: "Tools for the intelligent gambler"; online catalog shopping for just about any poker book, video, or computer program out there.

www.pokerpages.com: A comprehensive site featuring articles, tips, tournament information, card room directories, online play, and much more.

www.twoplustwo.com: Here you'll find excerpts from books by David Sklansky, Mason Malmuth, and others, plus discussion groups and strategy forums.

www.vorza.com: John Vorhaus presents *Vorza's Brain*. Self-indulgence is its own reward.

SOFTWARE

Good poker simulations are indispensable to the serious poker player, as is good record-keeping software. Some of my personal favorites include:

StatKing and *Card Player Analyst:* Both offer comprehensive record-keeping and results-analysis features.

Mike Caro's Poker Probe: Want to know how T-9 suited stacks up against A-3 offsuit over a million hands or so? All your answers are here.

Turbo Texas Hold'em: This Wilson Software product allows you to simulate hold'em play for fun or study. Wilson offers *Turbo* simulation for Omaha, seven-card stud, and other games, as well as tournament configurations.

About the Author

John Vorhaus has been writing about poker since 1988. His columns, commentary, articles, and fiction have appeared in *Card Player, Poker World, Poker Digest, Casino Player,* and other publications. He is the author of *The Pro Poker Playbook: 223 Ways to Win More Money Playing Poker.* In the non-poker realm, he writes screenplays, teleplays, and books including *Creativity Rules!* and *The Comic Toolbox: How to Be Funny Even if You're Not.* He also travels and teaches worldwide on subjects ranging from story development to creative problem solving. John lives in California with his wife, Maxx Duffy, and his dogs, Dodger and Ranger, and he dwells in cyberspace at www.vorza.com.